Billion Dollar Blueprint

Praise for *Billion Dollar Blueprint*

"What really excited me about discovering this asset class is the ability to earn an exceptional rate of return while still having safety, security and true asset protection. Plus no management fees or market risk. Coming from the banking world, this is like a dream come true. There is a reason why the major institutional investors and people like Warren Buffet have been using this product for decades."

--**Peter Viater**, former Community Bank President of M&I Bank Ashland, Wisconsin

"Stephen has such an intense knowledge of what most would say is an outside of the box strategy. I have made it my duty to always be in search of what could benefit my clients in the best way and I feel a life settlement accomplishes that. A life settlement is the ultimate way to secure peace of mind when building a smart retirement plan."

--**Ashley Wyrick**, Safe Money Group Indiana

"I have been in the financial services business for 30 years. In my opinion Stephen Gardner ranks at the top. He is tireless and resolute in his efforts to find safe ways to build wealth. Life settlements is a unique wealth accumulation vehicle primarily used by large institutions. Using life settlements in your portfolio is a great way to control the growth of your wealth predictably and systematically. Stephen's ability to explain this concept simply and concisely is out of this world."

--**Rick Kelley**, Safe Money Solutions. New York and New Jersey

"If there's one person I trust, when it comes to understanding life settlements, it is Stephen. He has taken his research and study to another level on an asset class that can be so beneficial for people looking for safety, good returns and peace of mind."

--**Brian Lund**, Author of "**The Millionaire Safety Secret**"

“Stephen Gardner’s deep knowledge and understanding of the life settlement asset class is matched with a driving passion to help both financial advisors and individuals to understand what life settlements are and where they fit in one’s portfolio. Over the past ten years my clients have loved the safety, security and peace of mind that they achieve with the retirement products I offer. Thanks to Stephen, I have added life settlements as an additional complementary offering to my sophisticated and higher net worth clients, and this has made me an even more valuable advisor to them.”

--Charles R. Watt, Castlebay Financial LLC. Sarasota, FL

“This book is a must read for anyone considering a safe money alternative to add to or to otherwise balance a portfolio. Stephen's diligent work ethic shines through in page after page of this valuable book. In an industry full of generalities, Gardner drills down to the specifics that make this asset understandable. In my 35 years in financial services, I have seldom seen someone work so hard to get it right. Clients sleep very well at night knowing that their fractional life settlements are safe from the market roller coaster!”

--Mark Marshall, Boston, Massachusetts

"Stephen’s understanding of life settlements is second to none. I believe life settlements offer clients a way to contractually increase their money without worrying about market downturns. After 30 years of being in the financial services business I have witnessed how big banks and the wealthy follow a blueprint for safely increasing their wealth. Stephen masterfully reveals that blueprint here."

--John P. Hayes, ChFC Eagle One Financial, Castle Rock, Colorado

"Stephen is the master of Life Settlements. Without proper education, this market could be difficult, and confusing. Stephen’s knowledge and insight make it a pleasure to be coached by him."

--Kenneth S. Feyers, Florida

"Stephen gives brilliant insight and a refreshing look at an alternative investment by explaining an approach that isn't tied to the volatility of the stock market. This is everything that I try to explain to my clients about the safety and power of life settlements in one easy to read book. I've been in financial planning for 22 years and this book sums up my approach to helping clients protect and grow their wealth. Thank you Stephen for a great book!"

--**Ron Weller**, Dayspring Advisors Group, Michigan

"Finally a trusted authority explains the fractional life settlement program in a simple way. This book is long overdue and Stephen Gardner is just the one to bring it to light. His style of educating through stories makes it so everyone can quickly grasp how powerful life settlements are for safely growing money. This book will open your eyes to an unseen world that will change the trajectory of your family's future. The book is a must read for anyone wanting to get their money out of Wall Street."

--**Paul F. Johnson**, Salt Lake City, Utah

"Stephen's knowledge and understanding of life settlements is impressive. His ability to explain an institutional investment in plain language is terrific. He has spent the time researching and compiling everything an investor needs to know about this asset into an easy to read book. I've been in the financial services business for 17 years and I've never come across an investment like this."

--**Darin Maughan**, Maughan Enterprises, Inc, Star, Idaho

"I was introduced to life settlements over 15 years ago. I have witnessed the evolution of this incredible asset, both for sellers and for buyers. Life settlements is a growing opportunity and for good reason. It allows investors to take their money off the Wall Street rollercoaster and earn potential double digit returns. Stephen's understanding and passion for this investment are incredible. He's truly dedicated to the well-being of his clients and advisors."

--**Joshua Schlinsky,** Safe Secure Financial, Inc. Florida

"Stephen's simplified approach and knowledge of life settlements has allowed me to give my clients the peace of mind they are looking for concerning their investments. Stephen's openness to share concepts, stories and lessons, has been invaluable to our group. By taking advantage of the safety provided by Life Settlements, savvy investors can get market like gains without the risks and fees associated with the stock market."

--**Rod Ferrier,** Harrisonburg, Virginia

"It's about time! For investors looking for a safe alternative to the Wall Street casino, your search is over. Industry authority, Stephen Gardner, explains what the banks and Wall Street have been doing all along. The Fractional Life Settlement asset class is explained in a simple to understand and easy to implement format. The book is brilliant! You won't live in fear of another market crash once you learn how to buy equity, rather than grow it. Thank you Stephen for shining some much needed light on this incredible investment alternative."

--**Morgen M Jackson**, Salt Lake City, Utah

"After 3 decades of providing safe money tools to my clients, I am excited to share life settlements with them. Stephen's book is powerful and clear on why we should be copying what institutions are doing. Read his book and let the light bulb go off in your mind like it did in mine."

--**Mel Aguilar**, RFC, California

Billion Dollar Blueprint

What Big Banks Don't Want You To Know About Life Settlements

By Stephen Gardner

ISBN-13: 978-1502597090

This publication is designed to provide accurate and authoritative information with regard to the subject matter covered. It is sold with the understanding that the author, through this book, is not engaged in the of rendering legal, tax, accounting, or otherwise professional advice. If legal advice or other expert assistance is required, the services of a competent professional should be sought. The author of this book makes no representations or warranties with respect to the accuracy or completeness of the contents of this work and specifically disclaims all warranties, including but without limitation warranties of fitness for a particular purpose.

The information in this book is for general use, and while it is believed to be reliable and accurate by the author, it is important to remember individual situations may be entirely different. Therefore information should be relied upon only when accompanied by individual professional financial advice. You need to consider your specific situation, including your financial goals before acting on any information presented in this book. Please know that neither the information presented nor any opinion expressed is to be considered as an offer to buy or purchase any insurance or securities products and services referenced herein.

No warranty may be created or extended by sales or promotional materials. The strategies and advice contained herein may not be suitable for every situation as all situations are unique. The author is not liable for damages arising there from.

Stephen Gardner, his employees or representatives are not authorized to give tax or legal advice. Individuals are encouraged to seek advice from their own tax and legal counsel. They are also encouraged to seek advice from their own financial and/or insurance and or securities professional. Insurance and Securities sales vary state by state and a professional should be sought after to fully understand the laws and regulations in each country or state.

Billion Dollar Blueprint

What Big Banks Don't Want You To Know About Life Settlements

Stephen Gardner

Foreword

When Stephen called me and said he would be writing a book on fractional settlements, I got excited. Why? Because he is one of the leading authorities on this subject and is a master of taking a complicated topic and making it easy to understand.

He's going to teach you a strategy that will energize you about building your wealth without the fear of loss. This concept may have a major impact on the way you and other families will save for retirement in the future.

Stephen is also going to give you an even greater gift – Hope.

Hope that, if you choose, you can start watching your investments and retirement funds grow safely again. Hope that you can look at your investment statements and not see losses. Hope that you can build a legacy for your children and grandchildren with money that can continue to grow for generations. Hope that you can go to sleep at night and know that regardless of what happens in the economy, the stock market, or world events; they won't affect this alternative investment.

We live in a turbulent world. Interest rates are down. Meanwhile, inflation silently erodes your investments and income. Boomers are worried that they will become dependent on their children for assistance. Some are even concerned they will have to work until they die, or worse, that they will outlive their money.

What if you could have a safe, simple and predictable investment that would eliminate all those issues?

The days of working one's entire life for the same company and retiring with a lifetime pension are gone. IRAs, 401ks and 403bs are a way to save for the future. But, they may not be the safest way to do it. In fact, the only people getting rich from those programs are the companies who lure you into investing in them.

Stephen will show you another way, life settlements. He'll pull back the curtain on how banks, foundations, and large charities have consistently grown their money using a strategy that was once only available to them. Even Warren Buffett, whose motto is it is more important to 'never lose money', has been investing in life settlements for the over a decade.

Stephen will show you how the most stable financial institutions in the world – life insurance companies - have given you an opportunity to participate in an investment so safe it's ranked in the category with CDs and treasuries.

Stephen gets it. He's spoken with hundreds of individuals who are concerned about the Wall Street roller coaster and the safety of their investments, and has steered them towards a new investment vehicle which provides the safety they seek for their investments. Because of his in-depth experience and ability to cut through the clutter, he will provide you with a clear picture of what is going on in the life settlement industry and why it is imperative that you protect yourself first. He'll also explain why you may not want to bet on the stock market in the future if you want to retire comfortably.

It's time to stop accepting sub-optimal results in your portfolio and worrying whether you will be offending your financial advisors. Can they really tell you what will happen to your investments five or six years down the road? Do they have an exit strategy for these assets? Can you afford to suffer a 20-30% loss on your money?

We know there are no perfect investments. Stephen does an incredible job of laying out the good and the bad to know whether life settlements may be a fit for you. That's one thing you can count on. It's your money and your decision. He just wants to make sure you have a clear picture of all the information before you decide.

Stephen has a big heart and understands the principle of giving. Whether he's working with other advisors, his existing clients, or prospects, his goal and passion is always to see others succeed and to see others helped.

My prayer is you read this book with an open mind. It may be the game changer you've been looking for to finally get peace of mind with your investments.

One final thought – imagine what your money will grow to and what your life will be like if you never have to worry about losing money again. This is not a dream; it's reality with the right strategy.

Mark Maiewski
Virginia's Leading College Planning Authority

PREFACE

I have heard it said many times, and have observed it first-hand as well, that the best way to make great financial decisions is to see what the masses are doing and then do the opposite. The wealthiest people in the world understand this and frequently go against the flow instead of with it.

Earlier in my adult life I was one of the lemmings that went along with the masses, letting the flow push us all along together. In 2008, after losing several jobs and seeing my 401k lose 38%, I'd finally had enough. As devastating as things were then, the losses set me on a path of monumental change; I'll never be able to go back to the old life and the person I once was. As of this writing, it has become even clearer to me that the way most of us were taught to save and invest isn't working. You don't have to look very far to see how true these words are.

Since those losses took place in 2008 and I began to make major changes in my career and in the ways I have invested, my life has never been better. My retirement account no longer loses money, and I have taken what I have learned as a result of my own mistakes and have embarked on a path to show others how to get similar results as mine. I have now worked with hundreds of families to show them how to improve their financial plans, and I've trained hundreds of other agents and showed them better ways to safely grow their clients' money. During this time I have researched and looked at numerous financial products and strategies, and after much investigation, I've discovered that many of them are both a complete waste of time pursuing and a complete waste of people's hard-earned money.

On the other hand, the strategies we will discuss here have never lost a penny of my clients' money. There is nothing sexy about these strategies. Many just have to be set in motion and left alone to do their work. I am grateful for these strategies that have allowed my clients (and me) to sleep well at night. It is also reassuring not to be receiving panicked phone calls from my clients about whether they have lost money or how a sudden drop in the market could send their retirement plan careening towards a catastrophic future.

Several years earlier, as I defined how my new business of helping people would operate, I mapped out my business and decided what criteria were absolutely necessary to hold my attention and be a part of my business model. When I found that there were products and strategies that offered safe and simple ways people could grow their money on autopilot, I was hooked. That was going to be part of my model. I loved that at no point could there be any chance for the stock market to steal my clients' money or take back the gains they had already earned.

I loved that these new strategies I found were also going to give my clients the gift of time. I could offer them freedom from having to watch the markets, freedom from the time they lost while glued to an easy chair listening to some talking-head on TV discussing the latest top ten list of stocks or mutual funds to buy this year. I could free them from worry and stress about the future while at the same time give them more time to spend with their families and loved ones and give them more time to serve others. Time is our most valuable resource. You can always get more money, but you can never get more time. With the strategies I am about to show you, I have been able to give my clients not only more money but also more time to enjoy it!

In this book you will learn about one of the few strategies for safely growing your money without having to watch the stock market, worry about the economy or lose sleep over your future. It's a strategy quietly used by the most well-known banks in the world to safely earn contractual increases on money without the worry of market volatility. I hope you will find this strategy to be as powerful and useful as my clients and thousands of other investors have. Once understood it will bring you the ultimate peace of mind.

Table of Contents

Chapter One

You've Been Kept In The Dark

"The problem in America isn't so much what people don't know; the problem is what people think they know that just ain't so."

--Will Rogers

"All truth goes through three stages: It is ridiculed; then it is radically opposed; and only much later will it be accepted as self-evident."

--Arthur Shopenhauer

The truth has been kept from you! I don't know of an easier way to tell you that you have been intentionally kept in the dark about how to safely and systematically grow your wealth. The tools that large banks and the wealthy have been using for over 100 years have been kept from you. Not only have these successful strategies been kept from you, but big banks and Wall Street have used marketing and educational materials to throw you off their scent, sending you down the opposite path. Why? One reason is so they can keep the money and charge you fees for storing it and managing it.

Have you ever wondered whether banks are making more money than they let on? That maybe banks are somehow making better returns than what they are sharing with you? Well, you'd be correct in your thinking! In fact, banks are making a killing while paying you peanuts.

There is a reason why banks make up the majority of the wealthiest businesses on the annual *Forbes* magazine list. There is a reason why bank buildings grow bigger and bigger each year. The simple fact is that banks tell you to do one thing with your money while they do something entirely different with their own money.

For example, Wells Fargo, one of the world's largest banks, in 2014 is offering .03% on their savings accounts and .5% on their CDs. These rates are so low they're laughable—except it's what they are in fact offering. Sadly, they don't even come close to matching our current inflation rate. How are people supposed to safely grow their money with such pitifully low savings rates? They can't, and so people are moving their money back into the same stock market that lost them 30-50% of their wealth in 2000-2002 and again in 2008.

While offering this incredibly low savings' rates, it's interesting to note that Wells Fargo posts incredible profits year-after-year. One of the ways they do is by purchasing what is known as Bank Owned Life Insurance or BOLI as well as life settlements. BOLI is a form of permanent life insurance purchased by banks where the bank is the beneficiary and/or the owner. This form of insurance is a tax shelter for the administering bank, as it is a tax-free funding scheme for employee benefits. Banks buy BOLI by the truckload. As of 2012, they owned a combined $137.95 billion worth of this kind of permanent life insurance. Bank of America is the largest owner with most recent data reports showing them to have $17.3 billion on their books.

Why are the most well-known banks in America buying billions of dollars of permanent life insurance to earn guaranteed returns of 4-7% each year while telling their clients to only buy term? Why is their behavior different than their professional advice?

Besides their purchase of BOLI products, why do banks also purchase and own billions of dollars of life settlements, and why do they also never mention these purchases to their clients? Why has Wells Fargo consistently earned double digit returns using the safety and contractual increase of life settlements and never shared it with their clients, the same clients they are paying .03%. Why, if you walk into a Wells Fargo bank and ask to be a part of their life settlement program, do their tellers and bankers look at you like you are crazy? It seems like they'd be willing to talk about it, since their ownership is mentioned on their own website. In fact, Wells Fargo is one of the largest sponsors of Lisa.org, which is the Life Insurance Settlement Association, a group n that has been in business for 20 years helping seniors get the most out of their life settlement transactions.

Protecting their Gold Goose

The reason banks intentionally keep you in the dark is because life settlements are the bank's golden goose that lays their golden eggs. Banks don't want to share the goose or the eggs. It's their secret fishing hole and they don't want you to know about it. They want to keep life settlements hidden, undercover, out of your reach, hush-hush. Did you know there is a hidden world of investments within banks and well-known financial groups? This is hidden world is where they place their company money, but you don't get to participate. They won't let you park any of your money there. Though you may consider this to be blatantly unfair because it puts you at a huge disadvantage, but it is reality. They make their own rules. You need to realize this is the real business environment that you are competing in. Isn't it interesting that while you worked with the bank to deposit your money and make your loans and pay their fees, you thought you were on the same team as the bank.

There's more. The financial institutions on Wall Street are even more secretive than the banks. They trade billions of dollars secretly each day in something called "Dark Pools". These dark pools allow institutions to trade large blocks of their own stocks completely off the radar and undetected by the rest of the market. As of 2014 these dark pools now make up 15% of all trades in the US. Billions of dollars are secretly traded here on a daily basis and your money is not allowed to play.

The truth is, why would these groups share a 100 year old strategy that can safely earn potential double digit returns with their clients when their clients will happily pay them high management fees to own an account that earns very little interest and is at risk on a daily basis? Of course banks and Wall Street would not want their clients to compete with them when they can control them as low interest earning clients. Banks and Wall Street stand as the middle man, making the lion's share on your hard-earned money.

Why has Merrill Lynch placed corporate money in life settlements for decades but has never made the same investment available to their retail clients? Why for over a decade has Warren Buffet been buying hundreds of millions of dollars in life settlements but not talking about it openly? Yes you can find this information in their annual reports and online, but if you don't know to even look for it, you'll never even know it exists.

So why are the largest banks, financial institutions, hedge funds and billionaires buying into this asset? Because of the safety of the insurance company backing the contract and the contractual increase they gain by buying equity versus waiting to earn it.

With traditional investments, you buy them at face value, hoping they increase in value or praying they do not drop in value. With life settlements, you are buying a guaranteed contractual payout from an insurance company for a discount and walking into a large amount of equity from day one. No guess work. No worrying about the stock market or the housing market. You are just buying interest in an insurance company's contract and patiently waiting to collect your share of the gains.

My purpose in writing this book is to bring this hidden asset class into the light. I want to expose a strategy used by the largest financial companies in the world to grow their money contractually. I want to show you a way to level the playing field and fire the middle man who is making a fortune off your money, while paying you very little in return. You've been kept in the dark too long. .

I hope you will find this information to be as exciting and powerful as I do. This is the asset that gets my clients wishing they had learned about it 20 and 30 years earlier. This is the asset that has my clients saying it's so simple and easy to understand. This is the asset that gives my clients the peace of mind that regardless of what the markets do over the next 5, 10 or 20 years, their money will contractually continue to increase over that same time frame.

As we get deeper into the mechanics of how this asset works, you'll see why it's so powerful to be buying equity versus hoping it will grow on its own. I'll share more about this in a coming chapter. You'll see why having an "A" rated life insurance company backing your assets gives you incredible peace of mind that you too can have the retirement you have been working so hard to secure. Lastly, you'll see how this asset is not correlated to the stock market. You'll see how your money continually increases instead of riding the ups and downs of the Wall Street roller coaster.

Chapter Two

Banks Blueprint For Buying Equity

"After 30 years of banking it's time America knew what the big banks have been doing. Life settlements have leveled the playing field for the little guy."

--Peter Viater, former Community Bank President of M&I Bank Ashland, Wisconsin

"Banks don't lend their money. They lend the money somebody else left there."

--Adam Smith

Big banks have a blueprint for safely and securely growing their wealth. It is a blueprint which is used to buy safe assets that inherently grow and provide returns regardless of the stock market, the housing market or the economy. Ironically, banks have tapped into one of their competitor's business models, to ensure their company dollars grow. Banks have tapped into the life insurance business.

Banks don't invest. They save! If you look at the way banks have grown their money for the past 100 years, it has not been through Wall Street. It's been through arbitrage and buying safe assets which have consistently grown.

So what do I mean by arbitrage? I mean that banks are earning a marginal spread off someone else's money. For example, banks pay their customers .03% on savings account and charge 4-7% on car loans. Banks do this all day long with other people's money to safely make a high return. Are they investing the money they hold for others? Nope! The bank turns around and lends the money to other clients who have high credit scores and have a high probability for repaying the money. When they do, they bank makes a tidy profit.

Banks rarely take chances, which is why they stay outside of the Wall Street casino. Wall Street is way too risky for them. Instead of playing in the casino, banks stick to their blueprint of lending other people's money to customers with good credit and buying into safe assets that are managed by life insurance companies.

So what are the safe assets banks will buy? We already know that they will allow customers with good credit to borrow their own money or other customer's money for a much higher rate than what the bank pays. We also know banks will lend on higher ticket items such as cars, RVs or a home. Why do they do this? Because if the customer defaults, the bank can keep all of the money which has been paid and repossess the car, RV or home, and sell it to another customer. The risk to the bank occurs every 30 days with an occasional 10 day grace period.

We also know, big banks like to buy permanent life insurance with guaranteed growth rates. Banks purchase billions of dollars of life insurance because of the safety, liquidity and guaranteed growth rates. The banks use the business model and actuaries of the life insurance industry to safely increase their money by a contracted, guaranteed interest rate year after year. For over 100 years this has been a superb way to receive a contractual increase on their money.

In addition to purchasing life insurance, banks also began to purchase life settlements as a way to get contractual growth on their money. A life settlement is buying an older person out of their contract and collecting the death benefit proceeds. It's a win for the seller and a win to the buyer. I'll go into greater detail in the coming chapters.

Big banks figured out very quickly that they could tap into the life insurance industry once more by purchasing life insurance contracts from people over the age of 65 who no longer wanted their policy. By purchasing life settlement contracts banks could bypass the time they used to wait to collect on the BOLI policies by purchasing contracts on older individuals. The banks could also bypass the fees which come with life insurance because the client had already paid for them. It was brilliant and completely legal. In fact, it has been protected by the Supreme Court since 1911. Today banks now use BOLI and life settlements to predictably grow their corporate dollars.

We can learn a great deal from big banks about managing risk and saving money. Banks have a blueprint for how to safely increase their money. Do you? A blueprint shows very precise plans for accomplishing a task or building a project. To ensure the task's or project's success, you don't deviate from the blueprint because it is exact and thoroughly thought out on paper.

Most Americans today haphazardly throw money into 401ks and investments without knowing anything about them. it. Americans have completely outsourced their retirement dollars to Wall Street and then wonder why they consistently suffer such large losses every few years.

You wouldn't walk through the doors of the Caesar's Palace Casino in Las Vegas with every retirement dollar you own, right? And yet, the vast majority of Americans have all their retirement dollars "hopefully" growing in the stock market.

According to Barry Dyke, author of the *Pirates of Manhattan*, life insurance companies were the primary custodians of America's money prior to the invention of the 401k. People saved their money with life insurance companies because it would safely grow year after year. The most well-known companies in the world (even small mom and pop shops) offered pensions to their employees to attract and retain top talent. Those pensions were grown and managed by life insurance companies.

So how are life insurance companies so safe? Life insurance companies operate under legal reserves. Legal reserve means that life insurance companies have to legally maintain so much money in reserve accounts to cover all of their liabilities, at any given moment. This means the companies have to have the money on hand to pay out claims and to keep their promises to their clients. These reserves are heavily monitored. If the reserves aren't maintained, the life insurance companies are put out of business. Keep in mind this never happens. If a life insurance company is struggling, it is purchased and taken over by a larger insurance company. Thus, maintaining their impeccably clean track record of keeping promises.

Some of the life insurance companies I recommend when helping clients use life insurance to build a completely tax-free retirement have incredibly robust legal reserves. One of them has $1.25 in reserves for every dollar they owe. Another has a $1.49 for every dollar they owe. This means that even if the country went into a tail spin and the company had a huge number of death claims, the insurance company would have an additional 25 to 49 cents in reserves, for every dollar they have committed to pay out to others. This is a formula for safety and being able to keep commitments.

Big banks saw that they could leverage the safety and stability of these life insurance companies to strengthen their own business and increase their own money. Many of the top life insurance companies in the world have been in business for over 100 years. Some have been in operation for over 300 years. These conservatively run companies have been protecting their clients' money and keeping their promises for over 100 years. Can Wall Street say the same?

During the Great Depression when the stock market lost 89%, when over 10,000 banks failed, when unemployment across the country was near 50%, and America was struggling during some of her darkest times, these life insurance companies kept their promises. They did not miss paying a death claim or the opportunity to contractually grow their client's money.

During World War I and World War II these companies kept their promises. During the Dot-com bubble and the Great Recession of 2008, they maintained their commitments to their clients. Life insurance companies have been the most stable and reliable industry in the world for over 100 years.

If you compare their track record over the past 100 years to the track record of Wall Street, Wall Street fails miserably by comparison. Wall Street has suffered major losses and upsets on average about every 7 years, losing trillions of dollars for clients, while lining their own pockets with client money, corporate bonuses and bail-out dollars.

However, there is one thing that Wall Street is better at than life insurance companies. Wall Street is better at advertising and marketing to you. If you've ever picked up a magazine or watched TV, you know this is true.

Wall Street has sold America on the idea of making it big. Wall Street has sold America on being OK with risk and losing money. Wall Street has sold America on speculating on what they will earn. Wall Street also collaborated with the government to invent programs like the 401k to systematically shift all risk to the consumer, while giving them the stock market as the only resource for growing money.

Wall Street has convinced us that investing and saving are the same thing. When money is lost, it is our fault for not being a better investor. Wall Street has convinced us that we should pay high management fees to someone for being smarter with money than we are; yet Wall Street has a verifiable track record of losing huge amounts of money. Think of how much you and your loved ones lost in 2008. Country wide trillions of dollars were lost.

Yes, Wall Street is better at marketing. In contrast the insurance companies that I mentioned have unbelievably robust and deep legal reserves yet do next to nothing when it comes to marketing. Instead these companies do word-of-mouth advertising and allow their reputation and track records to convince new clients to come on board. They aren't selling "hopium" in the streets or on every other commercial you see on TV. In fact, you may never see these life insurance companies advertising. These companies have chosen to spend that money on their clients, keeping costs low and putting that money to work in safe investments which have given them solid returns for over 100 years.

So who do you put your money with? The few funds forced upon you by your employer's 401k plan, the stocks the media and talking heads on TV promote, or perhaps the mutual funds claiming to average 12% returns.

Most people are not investors. Most people just happen to own investments and have outsourced their money to someone else. This outsourcing and lack of understanding of our investments has put us at the mercy of others. We don't understand the investments we place money in. We don't have an understanding of how the companies grow money. Ignorance is not bliss. Ignorance loses money and hurts our futures and families.

We believe we are investors because we own investments, but just because we pay someone to run the Boston Marathon for us does not make us a marathon runner. Just because we pay someone to build us a home, does not make us a homebuilder.

Banks are very precise about how they grow their money. Banks are very thorough when it comes to researching where they will grow their company dollars, and safety is at the very top of their list. Banks have a blueprint on how to safely increase their money. Banks work through contracts and choose assets which they know will increase their bottom line.

Success leaves clues and can be imitated. Banks leave clues on how to safely grow money. Banks lend money to vetted individuals with good credit or place money with life insurance companies within permanent life insurance contracts or by buying life settlement contracts.

Either way, big banks are banking on the life insurance industry to keep their commitments, just like they have done for hundreds of years. And so far, this strategy has made the banks billions of dollars. Don't be angry with the banks because of their blueprint, instead follow their lead and do as they are doing. Do as they do and not as they say. As the old saying goes, if you can't beat them join them. Work their blueprint to predictably control the growth or your money.

Chapter Three

Don't Grow Equity, Buy It

We have all heard the old cliché, buy low and sell high. It's great advice that almost no one follows. Instead investors tend to buy high and sell low. This happens because we are emotional humans who make decisions based on feelings, instead of research or information.

I cannot tell you how many people I have spoken with who bought a stock at the top of the market because it was hot or popular in the media, then sold the stock after the markets dropped, because of fear. Most of us have been victim to this emotion-driven behavior.

Truthfully, Wall Street counts on this happening so they can continue to make huge money off their clients, while taking little to no risk on their end.

What if I told you there was a better way to make money and it does not involve speculating or hoping the markets will go up?

What if you could walk into money from day one, and know exactly what you were going to make from an investment?

One of the ways to do this is to buy an asset at a discount. That way, you already have equity built into the investment. You are buying lower than market value and cashing out at a higher rate.

Let me give you an example that I share with my clients. I want you to pick between these two investment options.

Option 1: You buy a $100,000 piece of property and over the next 10-12 years it appreciates to $150,000 in value.

Or

Option 2: You buy a $150,000 piece of property sold at a discount for $100,000 and walk into $50,000 worth of equity from day one.

If you are like 99% of the people I speak with, then you probably chose option 2. It just makes sense to buy something at a discount and walk into equity from day one.

With Option 1, like many other investments or stocks, you are left **HOPING** the value goes up each year, and in most cases you are praying it doesn't drop in value.

It always brings me down when I speak to people who had money in the stock market from 2000-2002, when the markets suffered 3 years of back-to-back double digit losses or most recently in 2007 and 2008, when most people lost 30-50% of their wealth.

Losing money is the number one way to kill your chances of a great retirement. This is why Warren Buffett's number one rule of investing is "Don't Lose Money".

When you suffer losses in your account, it can take years to make up for those losses. For example, when the S&P 500 lost 38% in 2008, it took 5 years to get back to break even. This means you lost the opportunity to grow your money during that time. Imagine for a second where your account value would be today it you had not lost.

For most people it is like 10 years' worth of **actual** growth on their money vanishing. Imagine 10 years from now having the exact same amount of money you have today. It's a plan for disappointment and stress. It can be avoided!

So where are some areas in which you can buy assets at a discount and walk into equity? The first one that comes to most people's mind is real estate, buying and flipping homes. Another area is zero coupon bonds. The third area is life settlements. Although life settlements have been around for several decades, they are new to most people.

There are other areas where investors create niches out of buying at a discount, but let's just cover the three listed above.

Real Estate

Almost everyone knows someone who buys and flips real estate. This has been a lucrative way to make good money for a very long time. In order to make money doing this, you must find a home that has a sale price that is lower than the market value.

This could come from foreclosure, a family needing to move because of a job change, a short sale, or any number of reasons. An investor with money buys the home at a discount and walks into equity from day one.

As an investor you may even do some upgrades to get the value to climb even higher. When the home is sold, the investor takes the equity out as profit and rolls it into the next project.

This is a very hands-on investment with many moving parts and outside variables that could cost you the equity you thought you were purchasing. Real estate doesn't always go perfectly.

You could buy a home which ends up having significant problems that require additional money; money that you weren't planning on spending.

I have real estate investor friends who have broken even or even lost money on homes because of mold, flooding, leaking roofs, cracked foundation, termites, or because they couldn't get the house sold. Mortgage payments too ate into their profits. One of the worst things to happen is when the value of a home drops and its equity vanishes overnight. Sadly this has been experienced many times over the years due to house values changing with the ebbs and flows of the economy.

Zero Coupon Bonds

A zero coupon bond is a bond which you buy at a discount that has a higher payout in the future. Let's say you bought a 20 year bond with a 5.5% discount. You would pay $6,757 for the bond. The bond is then held for 20 years with a final pay back of $20,000 or a 5.5% compounded growth for 20 years.

This is not a bad way to safely grow money over a very long-term approach, as long as the bond market remains stable and soluble. You must also be careful not to tie your money up in something that is too long-term, because there could be a better investment option that comes along in a 20 year period.

Just consider where bonds, real estate, stocks and other investments were 20 years ago. Where will they be in 20 years? We don't know. But 20 years is a long time to wait and find out.

Life Settlements

A Life Settlements is a life insurance contract held on someone who is over the age of 65 who no longer wants to own his life insurance plan. The policy owner sells his life insurance contract on the secondary market for an amount higher than the insurance company is willing to pay him if he cashed out the policy.

Policies are usually purchased from the seller at 3 to 5 times the amount the insurance company would pay. The life settlements company is buying the fixed death benefit at a significant discount. For example let's discuss someone with a $1 million life insurance policy to sell. The policy would be purchased for around $300,000. This leaves $700,000 in built-in equity.

Ownership of the remaining equity is then sold off in fractions. So if an investor buys 5% of the contract he is contractually owed 5%

of the payout. Let's look at a real life example from one of the groups I currently recommend to my clients.

We have an 89-year-old female with predicted life expectancy of 40 months. If you put in $100,000 you are contractually obligated to receive $136,667 at payout. That means from day one you are buying into $36,667 in equity with a 40 month time frame of getting your money. The contract has a built-in return of 36.67% and over the predicted time frame, it will give an 11% or higher return.

So what makes life settlements one of the safest places you can place your money? One reason is that the payout comes from an "A" rated life insurance company. This means that independent rating firms have completed an in-depth research on the life insurance company and have determined that based on the way they run their business and the amount of funds they have in reserves, they have been graded at an "A" level and thus receive an "A" rating. These companies are incredibly stable.

Many of the insurance companies I use have been in business over 100 years old. These companies made it through the Great Depression and the Great Recession of 2008. By the way, there has never been a life insurance company in legal reserve history which has missed paying out on a legitimate death claim. Let me repeat that, **NEVER** has a life insurance company not paid on a death claim. That's a track record I can live with.

A second reason this investment is so safe is your money is in no way linked or correlated with the stock market. Your money is held in an escrowed trust account where the trust makes premium payments on your behalf until the contract matures.

Wouldn't it have been nice to come out of 2008 unscathed and actually making money versus losing years of hard work and having to wait another 5 years for the markets to break even? Stop using Wall Street's blueprint to build your retirement.

One aspect my clients have loved about life settlements is, knowing from day one exactly how their funds will grow, having a contractual increase on their money. This comes from buying fractional ownership in a contract that was purchased at a discount.

This gives clients the ability to make plans for the future and have peace of mind that as time goes by, they will arrive at their retirement goals. Did I mention that the payout you receive on your money is contractual? Not many investments can claim that peace of mind.

How nice would it be to have a clear idea of what your retirement funds will look like in 5, 10, or 20 years? Because life settlements are purchased with the same buying criteria year after year, you will know how your money will consistently grow over time.

With other investments, we rely upon hope as the strategy for getting to our retirement goals. Hope is a good quality to have, but a terrible investment strategy. Wouldn't you rather know your $100,000 will contractually pay you $160,000 in 5 years? Now that's peace of mind planning.

I started this chapter by discussing 2 investment options that were related to real estate. A unique feature of life settlements is that unlike real estate they don't lose value. So there is no worrying about property values dropping in the future. You own a fractional portion of a life insurance contract. If you have a $1 million life insurance contract, whether the contract matures in three months or 30 months, the value does not change. You get what you were contracted to receive as part of your payout.

What other investment tells you from day one exactly what your money will grow to, is contractually obligated to pay you that amount and will not lose value in the future?

What are your current investments contractually obligated to return to you? My guess is nothing. Instead you are told by investment firms and Wall Street that they hope they will return X percent. The only thing most investment firms put in a contract is how much they will charge you each year, and even then it's kept hidden.

As you plan your future and where you will place your hard earned money, consider the need to protect your hard work at all costs and to buy into assets at a discount so you have equity from day one. This will significantly improve your investment outcome by having control and predictability of how your money grows.

Remember, the wise man built his house upon the rock, not the sand. A rock is stable and sturdy. You can build on a rock. The sand is blown by the wind and sucked out to sea. You never know where it will end up.

Institutions have used a blueprint to build their own solid foundation. They have been using life settlements for several decades. These groups understand the value of buying low and cashing out high. However, these groups have been recommending inferior investments to their clients.

Stop losing money on investments, stop paying full price and stop hoping your money will be there when you need it. My best advice is to buy equity instead of trying to grow it. Growing equity has too many variables, too many things outside of your control, and too much uncertainty. You have too much riding on your future to follow the 'we hope your money grows' plan.

Why not instead buy equity? Bypass the stress that comes from watching the markets. Bypass the worry that comes with watching your portfolio go up and down like a roller coaster. I know you have either experienced the gut wrenching feeling of losing a large chunk of your hard earned money or know someone who has. Unfortunately, I speak with hundreds of families each year who have lived through this stress. Luckily, there is a solution to help them avoid this stress and heartache moving forward.

There is a better way to grow your money. Buy into contracts with built-in contractual values. How much peace of mind would it give you to know from day one how your money will grow? How much peace of mind would it give you to have an A rated life insurance company with a 150 year track record of keeping promises as the company paying on the contract?

Do what big banks and Warren Buffet have done. Buy equity in the safest, most stable asset on the planet, life insurance. Then collect the money you are contractually owed.

Chapter Four

Understanding Life Settlements

"Each day, each month, each year. 1 more, 1000 more, 1,000,000
more investors will gradually learn the foolishness
of this investment system and will start
looking after themselves."

--John Bogle,
Former CEO of The Vanguard Group

"Two roads diverged in a wood, and I—
I took the one less traveled by and that has
made all the difference."

--Robert Frost

"The greater the risk, the greater the reward." is a common saying in the investment world. It's most likely a saying made up by someone on Wall Street to lure investors into riskier and riskier investments, while at the same time giving themselves a Golden Parachute to escape any backlash with the old "we told you it was risky" excuse.

Who says there has to be huge risk to make a good return? I work with plenty of people making good returns with little to no risk. Knowledge and understanding of the investment are the keys. .

How hard would it be to win a sports game if the rules were constantly changing? Or how hard would it be to lay a solid foundation to build your future home on if the ground was constantly moving underneath you? It would be difficult and hard to stay ahead of the next move. This is the investment world in which Wall Street operates in on a daily basis and they haven't yet mastered it themselves.

Wall Street's dirty secret is, they gets paid to play with someone else's money, with someone else's dreams, with someone else's future, as they are learning. If you are tired of having the rug jerked out from under you, then life settlements may be the right investment for you.

A life settlement is a life insurance policy on someone 65 or older, which has been sold on the secondary market to someone else or to a company. Back in 1911, the Supreme Court ruled that a life insurance contract was a real asset that an individual had the right to sell just like any other asset such as land or a home.

With today's unstable economy, selling a life insurance plan has become increasingly more popular due to income needs and estate law changes.

Having 3 years of double digit losses in 2000, 2001 and 2002, did not set many baby boomers up for success or help those already in retirement. To add insult to injury, the market's tanking by 38% in 2008 and not growing in 2011 has left many people, seniors especially, wondering where they will derive the income they need to live on. For many, the answer has been life settlements, both as a seller and as an investor.

For the seller they are able to free up cash that was going towards insurance premiums and receive a large lump sum of money. For the buyer they are able to buy a fixed payout at a discount and walk into equity from day one. This eliminates the pressure to grow and protect money, while giving confidence that you will receive a contractual increase on your investment. This is a win-win for both parties.

Imagine trying to climb the stairs towards your retirement goals and every 5-7 steps is a trap door that opens and drops you down several levels. As children this was funny to watch on Saturday morning cartoons, but when it comes to our money it isn't funny. In fact, sometimes it can be devastating.

Have you ever wondered or even calculated where your money would be today if you had never lost? My guess is you would be significantly further ahead. Most people chase big returns because they know they will have to make up for years where they lost money.

What if you could get good returns but be protected against loss? I recently had one of my largest investors say something to me about his opinion on using life settlements as part of his investment portfolio.

My client said, "The reason I like investing in life settlements is because it reminds me of what investing used to be like. You should be able to understand the investment yourself, you should be able to do the math and you should know when you will get your money and earnings back. With life settlements I can do that and I understand how I will make my money."

Are your investments complex or simple to understand?

Has your financial planner shown you the math on how he is going to get you to your retirement goals or is he just using hope as a strategy? Most can't show you the math because they have no control over the stock market or economy. They are at the whim of the market just like you.

Do you have a clear idea of where your money will be in 5 or 10 years or can you not even begin to calculate what outside influences could throw you off track?

With life settlements, you know from day one how your money will grow. You know from day one what the time frame is and you see the math on how this is accomplished.

The reason you know this upfront is because the company will show you and walk you through it. If you take fractional ownership in a $5 million contract, that contract does not gain or lose value. The contract will be worth the same tomorrow as it will be in the future.

You are simply buying a pro-rated fraction that will pay the same fraction back, meaning if you buy 5% of a contract, you will receive 5% of the proceeds.

Let's look at an example together. Let's say you put $50,000 into a contract on an 84-year-old man. The contract has a built in 44% return. You know from day one, before you even buy into the contract, that your money will be returned to you at the new amount of $72,000. $50,000 x 1.44 = $72,000. This is the contractual amount your money will increase to. Remember you know this from day one and it is contractual.

What is not known is the exact day when the contract will mature. It could be in 1 year or it could be in 4 years. The life settlement company you choose should be able to provide you with the life expectancy reports on each of their contracts. The actuarial firms that are used to determine a life expectancy have high accuracy rates.

Although these life expectancies are not guaranteed, you know within a certain time frame when the contract will mature. It could be sooner or later or right on schedule. Your life settlement specialist will be able to share with you the life expectancy calculations, the age of the person when the contract was purchased, your contractual payout at maturity and your potential premium obligation if the contract goes long.

To determine your rate of return in life settlements you simply divide the built-in return by the time frame. Keeping with the previous example of a 44% built-in return, if the contract matures in year 1, you will make a 44% return. If it matures in 2 years, you make a 22% return. If it matures in 3 years, you make 14.6%. If it goes to the 4th year, it would be 44% divided by 4 years for an 11% return in each year and so on and so on with the math. Make sure to ask the life settlement companies about their targeted return. This is the criteria they use when purchasing contracts. Most companies will not accept or purchase a contract that does not fit their specific criterion.

The amount you will receive on a contract is predetermined. The percent you gain is built-in. The only moving part of this simple investment is time. Your $50,000 returns at $72,000 regardless of the time frame. Whether your contract matures in 30 days, 30 months or 48 months, you will receive what you contractually signed on to receive. This is the beauty of buying equity in a fixed payout.

Now compare that with a mutual fund made up of dozens and dozens of different companies and each of the companies moves at the whim of the market, the economy, and world events. There is nothing like an earthquake happening in Japan thousands of miles away to make your retirement funds here in America drop. The stock market in the United States dropped by over $300 Billion in a 72 hour period because of the 2011 earthquake and tsunami in Japan. You can't control the economy or catastrophes around the world, but they can surely affect your retirement dollars!

Life settlements should be a cornerstone in every investor's portfolio. An investment in life settlements minimizes the volatility of your portfolio because they are not correlated to the stock market, bonds or any geo-political events, government shutdown, threats of war, or cities filing for bankruptcy. Life settlements stand on their own because of the relationship with insurance companies and the payout being tied to an individual contract.

A life settlement investment brings peace of mind, so you won't wake up one day to news that the markets have crashed again due to some event, dot-com bubble, mortgage bubble, European financial collapse, a Middle Eastern war or the quantitative easing bubble we are in now, thanks to the Fed printing $85 billion a month to prop up the stock market.

The older we get the more important it is to avoid major setbacks in our retirement accounts. Most people simply don't have time to recover from market losses. Owning an asset that is not correlated to the stock market gives you peace of mind and provides uninterrupted growth on your retirement account.

So how does interrupted growth affect your retirement account? Let's say you have $100 and you lose 50%. You now have $50. Now let's say that tomorrow you get 50% back. How much do you have? Most people are inclined to say $100, but actually you only have $75.

You see the 50% you earned the next day is on your new, lower amount of $50. You would actually need a 100% return just to get back to break even on the original $100 you started with. That's why when the market drops it hurts for a long time. It can take 5 to 10 years to claw back to where your account values were prior to taking a loss. Market loss can cost you decades of savings and time. Plus leave you needing much larger returns to get back to break even. Let me illustrate in the table below what is needed to make up for a loss.

Percent needed to get back to break even after market loss:

Percentage lost	Percentage needed to break even
-20%	25%
-30%	43%
-40%	67%
-50%	100%
-60%	150%
-70%	233%

The table above makes it very easy to see why it took 5.5 years for the S&P 500 to climb back to break even after losing in 2007 and 2008. I know it seems crazy to show a 70% loss in the table, but from 2007 until the market hit bottom the stock market witnessed a 52% drop. During the Great Depression the stock market dropped by 89% and took 22 years to recover from the losses. Losing money wreaks havoc on your accounts and steals the time your account needs to compound your money. The interruption caused by loss can rob you of hundreds of thousands of dollars in retirement. On average the markets drops every 5 to 7 years and can take 5 to 7 years to break even. Sometimes they break even just in time to lose again.

We saw this in 2008, 2001, 1994 and 1987. There is a definite pattern to be seen. If history holds true 2015-2016 could be a rough time to be gambling in the markets. Life settlements provide an ideal environment for safely growing money outside of the stock market.

Characteristics of an ideal investment

I'd like to share a few reasons why I believe life settlements are an ideal and safe investment.

Performance:

From the *The Wall Street Journal*, to *Forbes Magazine*, to *Bloomberg*, to *The Huffington Post*, to *Affluent Magazine*, and to many university studies such as those done by The London School of Business or The Wharton School of Business, all sources discuss the 12% or higher returns the life settlement asset class has provided.

It's no wonder Warren Buffet's Berkshire-Hathaway, Bank One, Bank of New York, Barclays, Chase, Citi Group, Deustche Bank, GE Capital, Morgan Stanley, Wells Fargo, Price Waterhouse Coopers, Royal Bank of Scotland and Merrill Lynch have all used this asset class to prop up and stabilize their portfolios. These groups want safe, simple and predictable returns. A life settlement investment provides what they are looking for.

Safety:

Life settlements are considered a stable value fund and lie between money market accounts and investment grade bonds on the risk continuum. Returns are not correlated to the stock market or world events. Returns are linked to an individual contract which is backed by the most financially stable industry in the world.

Security:

Life settlement groups are monitored by and report to the SEC. They also use qualified escrow affiliates with experience in using collective trusts to manage and protect funds. Do not use a life settlement firm that manages your money in-house. Only work with companies that use a reputable third party account fund managers. Life settlements are also paid out by life insurance companies that maintain high legal reserves. They have never missed paying a death benefit claim. Only invest with a life settlement company that uses "A" rated insurance contracts.

No Management Fees:

There are no management fees or ongoing percentage cuts for managing your investment. The group you invest with is compensated during the policy acquisition phase and upon payout just like the investors themselves. This means all monies you allocate into life settlements participate in the investment. If you allocate $100,000, all $100,000 participates.

In the event that qualified funds are used such as an IRA or 401k, there is an annual custodial fee of $100-$500, for paperwork and reporting to the IRS. This keeps fees from devouring your growth. Your life settlement specialist will be able to provide you with the custodial fees on your account.

Liquidity:

Although life settlements are not a liquid investment like a savings or checking account, the investment time frame is typically 3 to 6 years. Upon maturity of a contract, investors may move their funds if they so choose. This is a good investment for retirement dollars that have time to grow and season.

This should not be looked at as a short term savings plan. Time frames differ, as each contract is its own investment and pays out individually. In the case of IRA accounts, investors will need to be mindful of their Required Minimum Distribution that begin at age 70 1/2.

Clear Exit Strategy:

One of the most difficult things about investing in the stock market is timing the market; knowing when to get out and when to hold out further.

With life settlements, you do not have to time anything. Your principle is protected and you will know from day one what the time frame is on each contract.

Life expectancy reports are used to determine when a contract will mature. The reports are based on medical history, age of the individual and the seller's current health situation.

Most contracts have a time frame of 3-6 years. You decide which contracts to purchase. Your specialist will help you determine which contracts are best based on your time frame and goals.

Easy to Understand:

Life settlements are easy to understand and so is the math. You are buying a contract that has a fixed future value which does not change.

You are buying a fraction of that fixed payout at a discount, knowing it will have a much higher payout in the future. The seller of the contract is using their life insurance contract like a reverse mortgage. The seller is pulling money out of the asset while they are alive.

It's a win-win opportunity because you are helping someone to profitably exit their contract while at the same time placing yourself in a position as the beneficiary of the contractual payout.

Conclusion

Life settlements are not for everyone. They are especially not appropriate for anyone that believes someone will live forever. Life settlement companies usually use two outside actuarial firms, with high accuracy ratings, to review the medical testing and background of the contract before it is purchased and made available to investors.

These time frames, although not guaranteed, are incredibly accurate and helpful when determining which contracts to place your investment in. Your life settlement specialist should be able to help you select the contracts and time frame most appropriate for your unique goals and situation. You want to only work with a group that will provide you with the written life expectancy report, so you can review them yourself.

One last thought--I have mentioned many big names and large institutions that buy into this asset class, yet these groups don't make life settlements available to their clients or investors directly. The group I choose to work with is a buyer of life settlement contracts and has large banks, trusts and charities as their clients. They also have an arm of their business that is wholesale to individual investors. In order to be involved in this asset you must work with a group that allows individual investors to participate.

Buying into life settlements means you are able to directly invest in the same asset class that many banks and large institutions use without the middleman taking their cut. You can now invest where the big banks invest. We all know that banks and large investment groups are making much more than they share with their clients. They would go out of business if they didn't.

Through life settlements you are able to level the playing field and buy into this phenomenal asset on a wholesale level, giving you access to the potential double digit returns this asset has been returning. No longer do you have to rely on banks and Wall Street for ways to safely and contractually increase your money. You have their billion dollar blueprint to follow It is easy to see why banks and Wall Street place billions of dollars in life settlements.

Chapter Five

Cashing In On A Hidden Asset

"Life insurance companies love it when someone over the age of 65 or 70 cancels a life policy. It frees up their reserves, turns the policy into a profit center, and eliminates a future liability."

--David Isaacson, author of Understanding Life Settlements

Imagine if in your 70s or 80s you discovered an incredible treasure that had been under your nose your whole life. What if you realized that a tool you purchased many, many years ago actually had incredible value?

I'm not talking about finding an antique or a unique object that you took to the *Antique Roadshow* and were shocked to learn it carried enormous amounts of value.

I'm talking about an asset that we are all incredibly familiar with. An asset that our parents used, that our grandparents and great grandparents have used. In fact, an asset that has been around for hundreds of years. What if you suddenly realized your life insurance policy was worth a significant amount of money to you while you were alive.

What if the life insurance company you bought your life insurance policy from had no procedure in place to educate their clients on using this asset in their later years? What if in fact, the life insurance companies worked very hard to make sure you never discovered your policy had value during your lifetime?

Wouldn't you want to know if the assets you hold are worth more than you thought they were?

Through life settlements people over 65 who own life insurance policies can now sell their policies on the secondary market, often for a significantly larger amount of money than the cash value they have accumulated. Lots of people, who previously thought they knew and understood life insurance, were surprised to find out about life settlements; they quickly determined it was a truly incredible asset class.

As this chapter will explain a growing number of Americans believed they had no other options with their life insurance plan. Rather they thought they had only two options: to continue to pay premiums until they died, or to surrender the policy back to the issuing life insurance company.

With life settlements, the secondary market has opened up an incredible way for Americans to take advantage of the safety and business model of the life insurance companies. Life settlements offer a reasonable and profitable exit from the life insurance contract which the insured may not want, or need, or can't afford any more in their later years. This truly unlocks a hidden asset.

Perhaps you've had a change in priorities, your life has turned out differently than you expected, or you simply don't need life insurance anymore, because your children are grown and successful. Many policy owners are now using a legally protected way to sell their life insurance policy on the secondary market just as it was intended and sanctioned by the Supreme Court over 100 years ago.

Having the option to sell your life insurance policy has created significant amounts of freedom for many Americans. It’s similar to having a healthy secondary market for selling homes and cars. Being able to sell your life insurance policy on the secondary market has been an incredible opportunity for improving the lives and the families of those wishing to sell their life insurance plans.

Let me set the landscape for why someone in their 80s would be open to selling their life insurance policy. Roughly 10 or 15 years ago when retirees decided to officially leave the workforce and retire, savings accounts were earning 5% interest, CDs were doing exceptionally well, and the stock market was regularly producing good returns. At the same time, the housing market was incredibly healthy and homes appreciated on a set schedule that people could count on.

In 2008, as the credit debacle and mortgage fiasco came into full swing, many seniors in their mid-70s to mid-80s were left with gaping holes in their retirement portfolios.

From the beginning of the market correction in 2007 until it touched bottom, the stock market dropped a total of 52%.

Seniors, dependent on their nest egg for income at this time, simply did not have the resources or the time to wait out the stock market and to make up for the losses in their retirement accounts.

To add insult to injury, the Fed and worldwide financial sectors lowered interest rates to all-time lows. As of writing this book, most banks only offer to pay you .1% on your savings account.

This left many seniors without a way to safely grow their money with any kind of decent returns. The stock market was no longer reliable and many people were significantly upside down in their mortgages because house values had plummeted. Banks were offering interest rates at all-time lows. Unfortunately, the low interest rate persists to this day.

The only asset that had not changed for these seniors during this time frame was their permanent life insurance plan. After meeting with their skilled financial advisor and discussing the original reasons for purchasing their life insurance plan and the reasons for holding onto it now. For many retirees it made sense to sell their policy, and exchange it for a lump sum of money while they are alive.

During this time, policy holders wanted to know if there was a more attractive alternative to simply surrendering their life insurance policy to the issuing life insurance company.

Reasons for abandoning or selling a life insurance policy

The policy is no longer needed or wanted.

As life circumstances change in some situations, life insurance may no longer be needed, it may become cost prohibitive, or it may be no longer wanted. Perhaps, the person named as the beneficiary is no longer in need of the death benefit money. The beneficiary may have grown up and become successful. Perhaps, the policy was originally purchased to provide for a spouse after the breadwinner passed away and the breadwinner has outlived the beneficiary.

Maybe the seller owns multiple life insurance policies or has chosen to keep one that makes sense and is financially affordable; discarding from their portfolio, the policy that is not. Sometimes, there is the opportunity to purchase a more affordable insurance policy with their proceeds.

In some cases, the seller can take the lump sum of money they receive for their policy and apply a portion of it towards purchase of a single premium death benefit policy. They then take the remaining difference and put it back to work in other investments, pay off debt or medical bills, thus providing for one's self and avoiding becoming a burden on their adult children and grandchildren. This option really allows people to maintain their dignity and remain self-sufficient.

Premium payments have become unaffordable.

Many of the policies I have worked with have death benefit values of $1 million, $5 million, or $10 million, and they also have expensive annual premiums to keep the policies in force. To maintain these premiums can become very expensive to a single policy owner.

However, by spreading the financial responsibility over hundreds of investors, the annual premiums become very affordable again. In some cases, an investor will sell partial ownership in his death benefit proceeds. He will keep 50% and sell 50%. Each case is different and each settlement company has different acquisition procedures and requirements.

Changes in estate planning needs

The US government is constantly changing the death and estate tax requirements. Most recently with American Tax Relief Act of 2012, the combined estate value for the death and estate taxes rose to $10,500,000 dollars, disqualifying most Americans from this tax. As a result, these high death benefit life insurance policies are no longer needed to cover the tax burden that would be placed upon the family members in charge of the estate. There is no need to carry an expensive policy to cover an estate tax that no longer applies.

Rising healthcare costs

Healthcare has increased and grown at a faster rate than inflation. With Obamacare, Medicare and Medicaid constantly changing what they will and will not cover, the financial burden ultimately rests upon seniors. In order to help ensure that seniors can maintain the quality of lifestyle to which they have grown accustomed and to be able to maintain their own health, having additional funds on hand helps alleviate the stress that comes from money worries.

Whether you own a term life insurance plan or a permanent life insurance plan like universal life or whole life, for many people at some point in the future holding and maintaining the policy does not make sense. Life changes, circumstances change and many times the original reason a policy was purchased does not continue as planned.

Most life insurance companies offer no viable exit strategy

Based on most people's understanding of life insurance, the only possible solutions for exiting a life insurance contract were to let the policy lapse and lose the money inside of the plan or to sell the policy back to the issuing life insurance company at whatever value the company deems appropriate; usually the cash value inside the plan.

If the policy lapses or cancels, insureds run the risk of losing the time and money they have paid into the contract. If they sell back their policy or surrender the policy typically they will receive a payout of 3 to 5% of whatever the death benefit is or the cash value built up inside of the contract at the time the seller wishes to part with the policy.

There is no reason to hold onto an unattractive policy or a policy that is no longer needed because of changes in someone's life. I remember when I was growing up, my parents used to rent their phone from the AT&T store. At the time, they needed a phone and this was the only option available. As phone technology improved and the cost of phones came down, it made sense for my parents to purchase their own phone, eventually moving completely to cell phones because the cost was so much lower. As life changed so did they. This happens with cars, homes and yes, life insurance needs.

Life settlements as a solution

By becoming familiar with and understanding life settlements, consumers now often have a much better alternative to simply lapsing or surrendering their life insurance policy.

Consumers who now chose to sell their policy in a life settlement transaction do so because they receive significantly more money for the policy while they are alive than they can by letting it lapse or surrendering their policy back to the issuing life insurance company.

By using a life settlement company, sellers typically earn 3 to 5 times the amount of money they would have received from the insurance carrier directly. Selling a life insurance policy can be incredibly useful and helpful to someone in their later years.

Another Secondary Market

Imagine if the only place you could sell your used car was to the dealership from which you originally purchased it. After 10 years of owning it, putting wear and tear on it, and driving it all over town, do you think the car dealer will offer you what you paid for it originally or will he offer you the lowest possible amount? The answer's obvious and this is why a secondary market is so important to car owners.

Let's say in 2004 you purchased an Audi A8. You wanted to own a fancy car that could go really fast, and yet was good on the snow and ice because of its all-wheel drive feature. For 10 years you loved that car and drove it everywhere. After owning the car for 6 years you married the love of your life.

Over the next few years you had a job change that took you to Austin, Texas. Two children were born. Life was certainly heading in a different direction. You didn't need the all-wheel in Texas because they don't get heavy snow. What you do need is a reliable car that can hold your growing family and their friends. So you decide to sell the car, and pick up an SUV that will be more in line with your needs and lifestyle.

The first thing you do is go to a local Austin car dealer to see how much the car dealer will offer you on the Audi as a trade-in. After inspecting the car, the dealer offers $4,300. You felt it was fair, but you wanted to see what you could sell the Audi for on the secondary market.

After more research and looking up the value and what similar Audi A8s were selling for on the internet you realize that it can be sold for between $6,900 and $9,000; the wide range depended upon what someone was willing to pay for it. You decide that maybe selling your car on the secondary market will benefit you more than trading it in and selling it to the dealer. After a couple of weeks and several showings, a couple heading to Montana makes you an offer on the car for $8,500.

After looking up the value and what similar Audi A8s were selling for on the internet you realize that it can be sold for between $6,900 and $9,000, depending on what someone is willing to pay for it. You decide that maybe selling your car on the secondary market will benefit you more. After a couple of weeks and several showings, a couple heading to Montana makes you an offer on the car for $8500.

The offer is not quite double what the dealership offered you, but it was a good price and it saved the other couple $2,200. That's the difference between what they would have had to pay the dealer and what they actually paid to you by buying it on the secondary market. This is a win-win deal both for the seller of the Audi and the Montana couple, the buyer; this is all thanks to a healthy secondary car market.

By trading it into the dealership, you would have received value for your car and you would never have known that you were leaving a lot of money on the table. . But by asking around and doing some research, you realized your car was worth much more than expected. The car had higher value to someone looking for a good deal on a car.

The same is true of life settlements, except we have to add on some zeros. Imagine you purchased a $10 million life insurance plan 15 years ago to take care of your wife after you passed away. Now fast forward those 15 years and you are now 85 years old.

Sadly your wife has passed away before you, and the $250,000 annual premium is getting very difficult to maintain without cutting into the money you need to live on. After being educated on life settlements, you realize, not only could you free up $250,000 a year by not paying the premiums to the life insurance company, but you can also get a lump sum of money to live on comfortably for the remainder of your life. After 15 years, you may have built up a cash surrender value of $800,000.

Life settlement companies, because of your age and health, may value your $10 million policy at $3.5 million. To the settlement company, your unwanted policy has great value and they are willing to pay for it. The seller ends up receiving over 4 times the amount of money they would have received from the insurance company. This is a big win to the seller. The policy had much more value to the secondary market than the insurance company was able to offer. Plus, it will give significant value to the investors in 5 to 6 years when the policy matures and pays out the guaranteed death benefit to them.

Key benefits of life settlements

Life settlements provide an exit strategy for an unnecessary and unwanted policy. With life settlements, a policyholder now has options for how to exit his life insurance policy. The policy holder can allow the policy to lapse, surrender it back to the insurance company or sell it on the secondary market for 3 to 5 times the cash surrender value. If you didn't want your life insurance policy anymore which option would you choose? Selling an unnecessary policy for more money is just a smart business decision.

By selling a policy, a consumer is able to receive a large lump sum of money to help cover the rising costs of living and other financial obligations without having to worry about running out of money. It gives them total peace of mind to receive this money.

Our lives, our goals, our priorities, our expectations, our concerns and our needs all tend to change on a consistent basis over our lifetime. These settlements help provide options to individuals for providing for one's self, by creating money from an asset during one's lifetime.

Life settlements provide flexibility, freedom and opportunity. By receiving a lump sum of money late in a consumer's life, he is able to use that money when his money may be limited.

A seller may choose to take their extended family on a vacation. They may choose to donate money to a hospital or university. They may even use that money to give themselves the time to work in a favorite charity or to assist those in need, while they are still alive to see the outcome. For most it allows them to live with dignity and not become a financial burden on someone else.

As I first presented the concept of life settlements to my own retired parents, my mother commented that her mother lived the last few years of her life in a qualified care facility. She and her 6 siblings had to pool their money together in order to give their mother the medical care and quality of life they felt she deserved. After a lifetime of giving and sacrificing they felt she deserved no less.

My mother then went on to say that she felt life settlements were a very kind investment opportunity because they allowed family members to take care of the elders and seniors in their life without having to deplete their own resources.

She said, "No one looks to get rich when their parents pass away, but everyone wants to see their mother or father have good medical care and a good quality life until they do pass."

Chapter Six

John and Mary's Journey

How do Life Settlement opportunities come about? The details are revealed in John and Mary's story, which is based on real people and real life events.

John and Mary had just returned from the funeral of a good friend who had passed away earlier than expected. John had known his friend most of his life. His passing left John with a great deal of sadness. The funeral caused John to reflect on his own life situation and mortality.

How much longer would he be around? Was his life in order? If he passed away, would he leave his wife and family in a good spot financially? After several weeks of reflecting on these questions, John decided that the $500,000 whole life plan he had purchased in his 40s would not be enough to take care of Mary should something happen to him.

So now at the age of 70, John set up a meeting with his insurance agent to look at purchasing a larger life insurance plan that would take care of Mary after he passed away.

John and Mary had always been hard workers and good with money. They had run a small gas station together for over 20 years. Even though they were both 70 and long past *normal* retirement age, they didn't feel they were in a position just yet because of the losses their retirement accounts had taken in 2000, 2001 and 2002.

During the first few years after buying the new policy, their lives had improved. The gas station had been good to them, and their retirement accounts were getting closer to where they had been before the dot-com bubble and 9/11 crisis rocked the world and their retirement plans.

Prior to these 2 cataclysmic events, in the late 90s, John and Mary felt like retirement was at their doorstep. Their retirement accounts had seen some of the biggest growth they had ever experienced. There didn't seem to be an end in sight to the increases they were seeing year after year. In fact, they started buying stock in several new companies that were hitting the internet hard and receiving lots of praise in the media. It didn't appear anything could stop the internet boom from rolling out and giving them the money they would need to walk away from the gas station forever.

That's when the dot-com bubble burst. John checked his statements in the mail as they came in. He slowly watched his accounts go down. At first, it wasn't a lot. The initial 10% loss seemed in line with what others were experiencing. John trusted his financial advisor when he told him to hold on and that the markets would come back. His advisor was right and by 2001 his accounts were coming back to where they had been in the late 90s.

What his adviser and the world didn't know was that two airplanes would be flown into buildings in New York City on September 11, 2001. John and Mary watched the TV that morning. They were sick to their stomachs that someone would attack their country. They were also sick to think about the Americans that were lost or killed in the twin towers as they came crashing down.

They felt lucky to not have any family in the area. They said prayers for those who did have family in this crisis. Wanting to help, they donated blood and money to the American Red Cross to help with the cleanup and the blood shortage that occurred.

At no time did it cross their minds to check on their stocks or retirement accounts. Even though they could not have done anything about it, it never crossed their minds that a crisis like this could affect their retirement accounts 1500 miles away. By the end of the year their accounts had dropped 13%. John and Mary had taken 1 step forward and 2 steps back.

By 2002, John's gut told him he should get their hard earned money out of the stock market before they lost anymore. However, he couldn't bring himself to do it. What if his stocks and mutual funds suddenly rebounded? He needed that money to come back, so he left his account the way it was because he trusted his advisor's prediction that the stock market would bounce back.

He felt it was easy advice to dole out to someone you were making commissions on, but this was his money and not the advisors. Despite his feelings, John kept his money in the market and hoped it would come back. By the end of 2002, he would live to regret heeding his advisor's advice. His retirement accounts lost another 21%.

By this time most of his hope had been sucked out of his sails. He wondered if retirement would ever be in the cards for him and Mary. After all, they should have already been retired by now.

But then the stock market began to improve and as it did so did John's attitude towards his future. His money had started to come back to its original amount in 1999, though he still had a ways to go.

Around this time the real estate markets started heating up, so John and Mary shifted their money away from Wall Street to focus on their gas station business, and they began buying and flipping residential houses. Initially this strategy worked and it was getting their retirement accounts into good shape. They had also opened a second gas station that was doing well and was profitable.

With their account values increasing every month, the two gas stations doing well and plenty of life insurance money in place, John and Mary wondered if maybe it was time to retire and start living the way they had always wanted, unchained from the business.

So in early 2007 John and Mary sold their businesses to a young couple looking to work an established business John and Mary made more on the sale than they could have ever dreamed when they first started their business over 20 years earlier. Life was really looking good. They had a savings account that was earning 5%, real estate that was growing in value by the month, and the economy seemed to be in growth mode. As they sold their business and started to pull their profits off the table, they again started investing in the stock market and mutual funds.

Things went well until late 2007 when the stock market started to slip and bounce around, but the real trouble started in the real estate John and Mary were holding. Property values started to drop, so the couple did their best to sell off properties or convert the unsellable ones to rental properties. This strategy seemed to be helping things; however; most of the properties they sold only paid them back what they had put into them.

As the property values continued to sink, stocks began heating up again, so John and Mary placed more money into the market. This time though they chose investments they thought would be safer than the ones they bought in the internet boom. They pick blue chip stocks and dividend paying stocks from large brands they knew and whose products they purchased.

Then, September 29th 2008 hit. The markets slipped by 777 points in 1 day. This set off a chain reaction that brought the markets down hard and fast. When the government decided to let Lehmann Brothers fall, a shock wave flew through Wall Street, then Main Street and then, the world. This triggered the Great Recession.

From the high in 2007 until the market found its bottom, the markets fell by 52%. In a 10 year period, John and Mary and most of America had lost over 49% of their wealth TWICE. “How could we be here again?” thought John.

The stress of losing their retirement money again nearly killed John. In the spring of 2009, John suffered a heart attack which hospitalized him for over a week. With all that had happened, he wished he had died, so his wife and family could receive the life insurance money and improve their lives.

John and Mary were never the same after this. It seemed there was no hope and no way to put the pieces back together. Luckily they had some money to live on, but at age 75 there weren't a lot of work options available. Jobs were already tough to come by with companies announcing layoffs and downsizing. They didn't have the health or heart to try to start another gas station, so they decided to cut costs where they could and survive this crisis.

John and Mary both decided that being in the stock market at their age was not a good plan. They thought it had been good to them, but it had also robbed them of their retirement once, and then robbed them again after they had retired.

They pulled out of the market and shifted over to a cash strategy.

However, the savings account that once boasted 5% annual returns was now only paying .1%. Returns on money market accounts too were low. CDs were low. Even annuities, once a good safe haven, now offered only low interest rates. Where could they turn for help?

As time went on, John and Mary decided they would keep their eyes open for opportunities. They would continue to the live the best they could and be mindful of their money. In 2011 they decided it was time to take a family vacation with their 2 children and 5 grandchildren.

They decided a trip to Disneyland would be a great place to build memories, and it wouldn't be too hard on their bodies. So they called the children and made the plans. It turned out to be one of the best trips of their lives. Watching their children ride Splash Mountain with their grandchildren was amazing. Shooting aliens on the Buzz Lightyear ride and then introducing their granddaughters to all the princesses were highlights of the trip.

After all, family was incredibly important to John and Mary. These memories would last a lifetime. After 5 long days of fun, they packed up and headed back home. It was a wonderful trip and never to be forgotten.

As thc months passed, money became tighter and tighter. On several occasions John and Mary considered dropping the $5 million life insurance plan. Mary felt she wouldn't need that much money if she was left alone and didn't feel the children would either. They needed the money to make sure they could take care of themselves.

After much pondering John decided to keep the plan. He felt it was his duty to leave Mary comfortable after he passed. He loved her so much, even after 49 years of marriage; the feeling to protect her and provide for her had not waned.

In late 2012 Mary's health began to slip. More and more money was being spent on medical bills and medication than they were prepared for. This led to late night discussions about whether they should keep the $5 million dollar life insurance plan. After all, John had a $500,000 whole life plan that was paid up. Surely that would be enough money for her to get by.

John confessed that the expense of the policy was draining them very heavily each year, but he wanted to take care of Mary. John knew how expensive nursing homes and qualified care facilities were these days and they would only get more expensive over time. Plus, they had only accumulated $300,000 in cash value. They had paid in nearly $900,000 at this point. John didn't want to lose the money he had put into the plan. He had lost enough already.

In January 2013 while having lunch with their daughter, Mary fell and broke her hip. . The hospital did their best to take care of her, but her heart had become weak. At 79 years old, Mary didn't have the strength to heal from her hip bone breaking.

A beautiful funeral was held to honor Mary. She had been a good mother to her children, and a good wife and business partner to her husband for over 50 years.

After the dust settled and life got back to some semblance of normal, John started thinking about the life insurance plan he had originally purchased in 2004 to take care of his sweetheart. Mary was now gone, but the monthly premium still had to be paid. He knew by keeping the plan it would place him in a bad spot financially and could eventually make him a burden on his children. He didn't think that was fair.

One night in late May, John invited his 2 children over for Sunday dinner and openly discussed his financial situation with them while his grandchildren played in the other room. He let them know what he had to live on and his monthly expenses. He let them know about the 2 life insurance plans and how much the larger one was costing him each year.

His children could see how the cost and stress would affect him and them over time. Neither the son nor the daughter was looking to make millions when their dad passed. Besides, they did not have the financial resources to take over the annual premium payments, while raising their children and putting them through college. After all, the annual premium payments were close to $90,000 a year.

As a family, they decided that it would be best to take the cash value and to eliminate the annual payments. This business decision would put John in a much better position financially. It would free him of many of the money stresses he had carried over the past 14 years.

Around this time, John's son read a magazine article about how seniors could sell their life insurance plan to a third party group and usually get more money than the insurance company would give. The magazine featured actress Betty White discussing the benefits of selling a life insurance plan for more than it was worth.

John's son decided to call on it and see what it was about. It was something called a life settlement. This group would pay his father 3-5 times the amount of cash value in the policy for selling the ownership rights. John's son learned that this was completely legal and had been protected by the Supreme Court over 100 years ago. Could this be true?

He and his father did a conference call with the group that week. Everything seemed to make sense, so John agreed to the medical exam and questions they needed to ask. Eventually he worked with a broker to find the company that would extend him the best offer for his policy.

After several weeks one of the groups came back and offered him $1.5 million for ownership of his contract. John was blown away by the offer. It was 5 times the amount of money he would receive from the insurance company. The payout would give John plenty of money to live on and leave to the children; plus he still had his original $500,000 whole life plan

After discussing it with his children and attorney, John accepted the offer and released ownership of the $5 Million plan to the group. The group would take over the payments, and John would receive a lump sum of money with a good portion of that being tax-free to him. This ended up being a big win for him and his family.

After selling the policy, about once a month John received regular phone calls from the buyer of his policy to see how he was doing and to get an update on his health. It wasn't at all intrusive. In fact, John became friends with the woman that called each month. In 2013 the family went back to Disneyland again to make more family memories. They wished Mary could have been there with them, but the trip was great fun and stress-free.

In 2014 John suffered another heart attack which hospitalized him. He quickly became weaker and not long after passed away at home under the care of a caring hospice nurse.

When the company called next to see how John was doing and get an update on his health, they could not reach him. They then called his daughter who explained how his health had changed quickly and that John had passed away. He was 80 years old. The caller expressed remorse for their loss. The daughter thanked her for always being so kind and for giving them several more stress-free years with their father.

The family would hold his funeral service the next week. Afterwards they sent the company John's death certificate, so they could file a claim with the insurance company. They also received advice on how to collect the $500,000 death benefit on John's other plan which they still owned.

John and Mary lived a great life. They had raised a good family whom they loved. They had created jobs for others with their company. They had been influential in their community. John and Mary were thrown some financial curve balls, like many of us, but they weathered these financial storms with dignity. When the opportunity presented itself, John was able to sell off an asset for much more than expected and gain value on it during his lifetime, which all helped him to cover his financial needs and leave his family in a good financial position.

This self-sufficient man had lived a good life. His family was grateful to the life settlement company for stepping in and helping their father live out the rest of his life with dignity.

Chapter Seven

Bill's Story: Finding Peace Of Mind

"Most people don't know whether they are investing, speculating or gambling, and to the untrained eye the activities are very similar."

--What I Learned Losing A Million Dollars
By Jim Paul and Brendan Moynihan

Bill was not having a good day. He was worried. In addition to a project deadline that he had been working on for over 9 months, Bill had broken a promise to himself, the promise of checking on his retirement accounts regularly. He checked that morning only to find that his account had dropped by another 11%. Because of the worry the stock market gave Bill, and the time he spent watching it each day, his wife had made him promise he would not check their retirement accounts on a daily basis.

The worry and stress was literally making Bill sick. It was affecting his ability to concentrate at work. Bill and his wife had decided to only check the accounts once a month. As of right now, talking about the family IRA money was off-limits.

Shortly after checking his retirement account, Bill's boss, Mark approached his desk, asking if he was ready for his presentation that afternoon. Out of frustration Bill snapped at Mark. Of course the project was finished and he would be ready to present. Bill's boss did not take kindly to the snippy response he had received to his inquiry. Bill quickly apologized. He told Mark he had looked at his retirement accounts earlier, and it had put him in a bad mood.

Mark mentioned that his accounts had been dropping also and that he was looking into some safer ways to protect and grow his money. Mark suggested that maybe later in the week; they should go for drinks after work and discuss what he had been learning. Bill expressed his frustration by saying that he didn't think anything was safe anymore and that he didn't know whom to trust. Bill decided not to go out for drinks with his boss.

As 2008 came to an end, Bill checked his accounts one more time before heading out to celebrate the New Year. He had lost a total of 41% of his portfolio. How could this be? "My advisor told me to stick with this plan and that everything would be okay. Now I've lost nearly half of my money."

Bill was sick and tired of all the old clichés like buy-and-hold, you just have to ride these things out, or the market will come back just you watch. Bill knew the markets would come back, he just didn't know how long it would take. At age 55 Bill was beginning to worry that retirement would not be in his future. He loved his job, but he didn't want to work the rest of his life.

As time went by, Bill's IRA account went up and down, following the trends of the market. He tried to make smart decisions by selling at certain times and buying at others. However, Bill's account didn't seem to get back to breakeven as quickly as he wanted.

During the 5 years it took for Bill's IRA account values to come back to breakeven, Bill realized that he had lost a significant amount of growth time on his money. Inflation had actually continued over those 5 years. The money he had earned back was now worth less than it was previously. This frustrated him. It got him wondering if there was a better way. Where would my account values be today if I had never lost? This question haunted Bill on a daily basis.

By the end of 2013, Bill's account had come back to breakeven. He even had more money in his account because of record-breaking returns. Bill and his wife were ecstatic at the growth they were finally starting to see on their accounts. Then one day, they read about how the Federal Reserve had been pumping $85 billion a month into the stock market. This made Bill and his wife question whether the growth they had seen on their money was real or if they had just entered into another bubble. If they were in another bubble, they were not interested in riding this next one out. They simply did not have time to weather another financial storm.

Because of the Great Recession in 2008, Bill had actually lost his job. He had to go find work at a competing firm. It wasn't until early 2013 that Bill ran into his previous boss Mark. There was a lot of small talk, chatting about old colleagues and projects that they had worked on together. Then Bill asked his former boss if he had ever found an answer to his question about safer ways to safely grow his money over time. Mark mentioned that he did have a few things that he felt very comfortable with and had participated in over the last 5 years. He had gotten involved in a strategy that made a lot of sense and had the ability to get good returns. Bill asked if he could cash in the rain check from 5 years earlier and go have drinks one night and discuss his findings.

About a week later, Bill and Mark got together at one of the town's more popular pubs to have a light dinner and drinks while they discussed the financial strategies that Mark had been implementing. After some small talk and catching up on each other's lives, Bill asked if Mark would be kind enough to share with him where he was growing his money. At the same time, Bill gave him some background on what he had been through over the last 5 years. He shared some of the worries and fears he had about another market crash.

Mark started by mentioning that he had looked into some strategies outside of the company 401k and his IRA for growing a tax-free retirement. He had done some research on Roth IRAs and had also discovered how the wealthy use life insurance to safely build a completely tax-free nest egg. Mark explained that while driving to work he had heard a radio ad that mentioned a strategy the wealthy use for protecting their money against market crashes. The ad also said that Mark could earn potential double-digit returns through a little-known way to build a completely tax-free retirement. So Mark said he called in for the free book that was being offered. It was mailed out to him promptly. At that time he also set up an appointment to speak with a specialist.

As Mark spoke over the phone with Andrew, the specialist, they discussed Mark's background and his frustrations and goals for the future. The specialist educated and shared some ideas on how to safely build a tax-free retirement. After feeling good about the plan, Mark decided to move forward with it.

Once the plan was in place, Andrew asked a simple question that got Mark thinking. Would he be open to learning about a strategy for his IRA, 401k or cash that was completely outside of the stock market and has a track record for safely earning potential double-digit returns? Mark said he thought they already discussed it. Andrew explained to Mark that they had only discussed one of the strategies that he had access to, but felt this one might be in line with what he was looking for based on their conversation and relationship.

This was when Mark was officially introduced to life settlements as a way of safely growing his money outside of the stock market. The idea made sense. Mark shared with Bill that he understood that he would be buying into a fixed asset, life insurance which had a guaranteed payout from an "A" rated life insurance company.

Mark said, "I also understood that I would be helping a consumer that for one reason or another did not want or need to own their life insurance plan any longer. I would be buying fractional ownership of a large life insurance payout. As I did the research and looked at the math, I realized that this was an incredible opportunity to help somebody unlock the equity inside of their life insurance contract, while giving me the ability to buy into a contract that would give me a contractual increase on my money. The only downside I could see was the possibility of the seller living longer than expected. However, I trusted that the company had completed proper underwriting and that the life expectancy firms which they used had a good track record for accurately predicting somebody's life expectancy. So I moved $100,000 over into an account, and I purchased ownership of 8 contracts. During the 4 years I have been involved in the life settlements program, I have had 2 maturities and been paid on them. The first was a 21% return and the other was a 15%."

Bill interrupted his former boss. "Let me see if I understand this, so you're buying partial ownership inside of somebody else's life insurance contract?" Mark responded, "Yes! The group buys the person out of their contract at a significantly higher amount than what they would have received from the insurance company. Then we patiently wait until the contract matures. The group collects the contractually obligated beneficial interest in the contract." At this point, Mark felt like he was not qualified enough to describe the whole process, so he thought introducing Bill to his agent, Andrew, would be in Bill's best interest.

Bill was a little hesitant to speak to somebody about his financial situation, but he trusted Mark, and so Bill agreed that he would meet with Andrew next week. Bill and Mark finished their dinner and drinks and parted ways with Bill holding Andrew's business card in one hand and in the other hand an audio CD which Mark had brought to the dinner.

As Bill drove home, he popped in the audio CD. The CD went through a recorded interview about life settlements, the history of the asset class, how the investment works, and how he could safely get good returns on his money during this low interest rate environment. And, he could do all of this without having to worry about what the stock market was doing. Bill admitted that he found the CD to be very interesting, but he was still skeptical and wanted to learn more.

The next day during his lunch break, Bill picked up the telephone and made a personal call to Andrew to introduce himself and ask if they could set up a time to meet.

Andrew answered the phone with a happy hello and asked who was on the other line. He explained that he was a former coworker with one of Andrew's clients, and it had been recommended to him to learn about the safe strategies Andrew recommends for helping his clients safely grow their money outside of the stock market. The two arranged for a time they could speak.

The next week Andrew called right at the time they had arranged for the appointment. This impressed Bill right away. The two of them discussed Bill's situation and what he had gone through. They discussed his worries and the things that he had read about the stock market. They also discussed Bill's goals and investing time frame. Bill was adamant that he did not want to be involved in another market loss.

Then Bill interrupted Andrew and said I'm specifically calling to learn about the life settlements program. I'm worried that my IRA money in the stock market will be lost if we suffer another market crash. Andrew said he was happy to jump right into the life settlement discussion, but had a question for Bill. Andrew asked Bill what he meant by "if we have another market crash." Andrew asked Bill very directly where he saw the stock market heading over the next 5 to 6 years. Bill laughingly mentioned that he did not have a crystal ball, but that he felt like we would see some market volatility and market corrections in the next 5 years. He then said, "I don't know if my retirement accounts can handle another 30% or larger drop at my age."

Andrew shared that one of the major benefits of a life settlement investment is that it is a non-correlated asset. This means it is not connected to the stock market. Andrew went on to explain that during 2008 when the market was dropping like a stone, none of the life settlement companies lost any of their clients' money because life settlements are completely outside of the stock market. Andrew then reminded Bill that the payout is based on an individual contract backed by an "A" rated life insurance company.

"So what makes this such a unique asset and how does it work?" asked Bill.

Andrew responded, "A life settlement by definition is anyone over the age of 65 who wishes to sell their life insurance policy on the secondary market. It has primarily been used by banks and large money managers for several decades and by the ultra-wealthy since 1911, when the Supreme Court sanctioned and protected consumers, affording them the opportunity to be able to sell their life insurance policy. The groups we work with specifically purchase policies on individuals that are 80 years and older. This helps control the time frame significantly. This is very different from large institutions which often will l buy the policies on any individual over the age of 65.

"As a policy owner decides that they no longer want or need their life insurance contract, they approach our group and ask to be bought out of their contract. The potential seller comes to us looking for a solution. Perhaps they need money to supplement their retirement, they've outlived their beneficiary or they just don't want to keep paying the premium payments. Our group is able to offer them a solution that may give them 3-5 times more money than the life insurance company can offer.

"For example let's say someone owns a $5 million policy and has $300,000 in cash value and this after paying into the policy for many years. When the seller wants to surrender the policy, the insurance company is only obligated to offer the cash value. However, sellers who work with knowledgeable advisors and life insurance agents know they can get a much higher offer by selling it to a third party. Based on the person's age and health, a group may offer the seller $900,000 to $2,000,000 for that policy."

"Why would a third party pay that much for a policy," asked Bill?

"The $5 million dollar payout is a contractual and fixed amount. It cannot change because of the economy, natural disasters or the stock market. It's a fixed amount, so by purchasing the contract for let's say $1,500,000, that leaves $3,500,000 in equity to the group."

"So I am essentially buying partial ownership in the proceeds of the $5 million death benefit." responded Bill.

"That's correct, Bill. Now you are starting to grasp the idea."

Bill loved the idea of getting his money away from the stock market. He also loved the idea of have a contract in place on how his money would increase upon maturity of the policy. He also liked that the group was using "A" rated life insurance companies. Bill had done some research prior to the call about life insurance companies. He had learned just how stable and strong these companies are. Some of these companies have even been in business for over 100 years.

Everything seemed to be making sense. The investment was simple to follow, unlike the mutual funds he was currently holding. Bill still had one question that he needed Andrew to answer, a question that had been on his mind since he had dinner with Mark. "If life settlements are such a great investment, then why haven't I heard of them before?" he asked.

This was a question Andrew received from everyone he had brought into the investment. It was an easy one to answer, but sometimes the answer wasn't what people wanted to hear. Andrew discussed with Bill how the Supreme Court in 1911 had opened the doors for the insured to be able to sell their life policies. He mentioned how up until the late 1990s only large institutions had been allowed to buy the plans.

In the late 1990s, however, the Fed's Securities and Exchange Commission, the SEC, decided that groups could start offering this investment to qualified investors. Most of the groups would use an irrevocable trust to buy the insurance contracts, and then clients could buy ownership in the trust. Trusts were used as a way to ensure the funds would be kept safe and that the companies couldn't run off with a client's money.

Andrew also shared how the company he represented was registered with the SEC as a 506 Regulation D company. This meant that the company could make private offerings to qualifying investors, but the company was not allowed, under any circumstance, to publicly advertise their offering. Simply put, the company is allowed to work with people they meet and know, but not allowed to actively advertise the company or product.

Andrew also explained how large banks and insurance companies have lobbied to keep this asset class hidden and out of reach of most people. After all, banks and Wall Street don't want their clients having wholesale access to the same products they do. Otherwise they run the risk of losing clients and gaining competitors.

This all made sense to Bill, but he still wanted to do his research. Andrew happily supplied him with third party articles and company information. An appointment was set to speak again in a week.

On the next call Andrew explained that he would tell Bill more about the settlement company and show him the current available contracts. Bill would be able to see the contracts, the time frame, the life expectancy reports and dollar for dollar how the money would contractually increase in each contract. Bill was looking forward to the meeting.

The following week when Bill and Andrew got back together, Bill still had some questions. "How do I make money in this investment? Also, the company disclosure booklet mentioned there is no annual rate of return. So how does my money grow inside of this investment?"

Andrew explained that there was no annual rate of return because there was no increase on his money until a payout came from the insurance company. Andrew then pulled up the current contracts to help Bill better understand the time frame and the math behind increasing his money.

You can see from contract number one, if you place $10,000 into the contract it will be contractually returned to you at $15,683. This is based on the pro-rated amount of ownership you've purchased. Andrew emphasized that regardless of when the contract matured Bill's money would increase to $15,683.

This got Bill excited. Now Bill could understand the importance of knowing how his money would increase while also giving him strong peace of mind. However, Bill wanted to understand what his rate of return would be. Andrew explained that Bill was really buying into a 56.83% increase on his money. Whether the contract matured in 30 days, 30 months or 60 months, Bill was contractually obligated to receive $15,683 or a $5,683 profit on his contract.

Bill was a little lost and asked Andrew to explain it again. Andrew pulled out his calculator, so he and Bill could see it together. This made Bill feel better. You see if we take the $15,683 you will receive and subtract out the original investment of $10,000 you will earn a $5,683 profit. Bill acknowledged that he understood that part now. Andrew continued by showing Bill that if you take the profit of $5,683 and divide it into the original $10,000 you get .5683. To get an interest rate, you multiply it by 100. Andrew's calculator displayed 56.83%. This was all making sense to Bill now.

Andrew pointed out that if a contract took 4 years to mature, then you take the 56.83% and divide it by the 4 year time frame. The calculator showed 14.20%. At this point Bill really liked what he saw.

Andrew interrupted Bill's happy moment to mention that this isn't a perfect investment. Bill asked what he meant by that. Andrew said he felt he needed to present the disadvantages along with the advantages. Bill had never worked with a financial planner that mentioned disadvantages, so he asked Andrew to explain what they were.

Andrew pointed out that the only moving part in this investment was the passage of time. He reminded Bill that this wasn't correlated to the stock market or the economy, but rather to an individual's life and that someone could live longer than expected. Bill asked what happens if the individual lives longer.

Andrew explained that at no point would Bill's principal or his contractual increase be at risk. It was just his ROI that could go down based on the person living longer than expected. . In other words more time would have passed than expected.

"So in this case, my $15,683 is not going to change, but if someone lives longer I have to divide by more years, is that correct?" asked Bill.

"That is exactly right, Bill. If the person lives longer, you have to divide by more years. For example, if the person lived 6 years instead of 4 then you have to divide the 56.83% by 6. This gives you a 9.47% return in each of those 6 years for a total of 56.83% increase on your money."

Andrew then explained that part of the $10,000 Bill would be investing would be set in an escrow account to make future insurance premium payments on Bill's behalf. Bill liked not having to worry about missing a payment. Andrew explained that on average the company places 7 to 8 years' worth of monthly payments aside, even though the contract may only have a 4 to 5 years expected time frame. A wide buffer of additional premiums is put in place. However, if the contract goes longer than the amount of premium set aside, then you as an owner have to send additional money to the company to keep the contract in good standing.

"So unlike the stock market where I was worried every year, for the past 7 years that I may lose my principal and interest, with life settlements I just need to be conscious of the premiums in escrow and that I may have to contribute additional money in the future?"

"That is correct," answered Andrew.

At first this made Bill a little nervous. It was totally new to him. After a few minutes though he piped up and said it made sense. After all, he didn't have to worry about losing his money or his return in that time frame. He just had to be conscious that 7 or 8 years from now, if the contract had not matured, he would have to pay additional premiums.

Bill said that this reminded him of his friend who got into trouble buying and flipping homes in 2007. His friend had purchased a large property to fix up and flip while the market was hot. As the market cooled, he had not sold the house, so he had to start coming out of pocket each month to pay the mortgage and expenses until he eventually sold the house at a discount.

However, Bill went on to add that there was a huge difference between life settlements and flipping houses. Bill wouldn't need to sell a house in a couple months and wouldn't have to worry about his contractual return changing with the economy. In 7 to 8 years from now he just needed to be aware of what his contracts had done. Andrew mentioned that with the group he used it was very uncommon, but he wanted to be transparent with Bill about it. Bill was grateful to know what to expect down the road before he ever placed any money.

Bill then asked if there were any other disadvantages. Andrew mentioned a few that seemed obvious but were worth hearing out loud. Andrew reminded him that his investment would not be liquid until the insurance company paid on the maturity. He also mentioned that this product does not provide a stream of income, but that Andrew would show him a way to create his own stream of income from the investment.

Bill was pleased that he could understand this investment before he ever signed any papers or placed any money. Bill knew exactly what his money would increase to at maturity. This made him confident that his money would grow every 4 to 6 years. He could actually make plans for the future. For the first time he felt at peace with his investments.

At this point, Bill was ready to get started and chose the contracts he wanted to own. He only had 2 lingering hurdles to overcome: how much money to place into the investment to begin and how to explain the investment to his wife. Andrew said that he would be happy to go through the investment again with Bill's wife on the phone. He also mentioned that he wanted her to fully understand how it worked and that Bill could decide on his own what he felt comfortable contributing to his account.

A few days later, after explaining to Bill and his wife once more how the investment worked and how it helped the seller by getting 3 to 5 times more money than expected and how their money would contractually increase, Bill decided to start with $100,000.

Approximately 17 months later Bill received a phone call from Andrew asking if he had a few minutes to talk about his life settlement investment. Bill replied that he did have time but that he didn't really have any questions. Over that time period Bill had continued to speak with Andrew, receive his newsletter and the occasional information CDs. However this time, Andrew was calling to tell Bill that there had been a maturity on one of his contracts. Bill sat in silence, not knowing what to say.

Andrew discussed with him one of the contracts that Bill had selected 17 months earlier. He reminded Bill how the contract had a 45% built-in return and a 4 year time frame. Bill had placed $20,000 into this particular contract, knowing from day one, that it would grow to $29,000. With a 4 year time frame, he was expecting to earn an 11.25% return in each of those 4 years, but because the contract matured earlier, the return was better and Bill could roll his money into new contracts if he chose to.

"So what did I end up netting on this contract?" Bill asked.

"Well, you will see $29,000 drop back into your investment account. Remember, regardless of when the contract matures you were contracted to receive the $29,000." Bill remembered this. "Since the contract matured in its second year, we divide the 45% by 2 years. This means you earned 22.5% in each of those 2 years for a total increase of 45% just as you were shown last year."

Bill was very happy. He then said something Andrew had heard before. Bill said, "I knew in my mind that it would grow to $29,000, but to have it actually happen is very exciting." He couldn't wait to share the good news with his wife. Bill couldn't wait to see the other

4 contracts he owned mature. Bill ended up reinvesting the $29,000 into 2 new contracts. He also moved another $200,000 from his old 401k into his life settlement account. Bill was very impressed and excited about his future.

Chapter Eight

Know It Before You Grow It

By this point, you're probably thinking this sounds amazing, but want to better understand how your money will contractually grow. Remember with life settlements, you are buying equity versus trying to grow it like with traditional investments.

When the life settlements company acquires the contract, the company has purchased the death benefit at a significant discount. By doing so, it creates equity from day one. **(Side note just to be crystal clear: the seller of the policy is not being discounted. The seller earns on average 3-5 times more money than the insurance company would give. This is a huge win to the seller.)** The discounted purchase is based on the death benefit.

If a $1 million whole life is purchased for $300,000, this leaves $700,000 worth of built-in equity behind. Depending on the cost to acquire the contract, such as legal fees, medical exams and actuarial fees, the contract may have a 50%, 60% or 70% return for the investor to contractually buy into.

The only moving part in life settlements is the passage of time, so once a contract is purchased, and the contractual return is posted, the clock starts ticking. To figure your potential return or your actual return upon maturity of the contract, you take the built-in return and divide it by the number of years a contract took to return your money.

According to a study completed by the University of London in 2013 on 9,002 life settlements contracts the University found the average expected return to be 12.5%. The 9,002 contracts represented $24.14 billion worth of contractual payouts.

In the tables below, I have given a basic idea of how rates of returns are calculated, depending on the contractual increase of the contracts purchased and the time frame.

I highly recommend that you only work with life settlement companies that will show you your contractual increase before you place any money. You want to be crystal clear on how your money will contractually grow. Also, only work with companies that provide up front information on the seller, will share the life expectancy report and the potential premium call, if the insured lives longer than the premiums set aside in reserves.

You don't want to be caught off guard with regards to this information. Get all of the information up front or don't place any money. For the seller's safety and HIPAA health laws, no life settlement company will share the insured's name or where they live, but they can and should be able to share their medical information and life expectancy report, so you can make a well-informed decision.

Again, the beauty of life settlements is really understanding how the money will grow and having everything completed by contract versus speculation.

The tables below will give you an idea of how money will grow based on the contractual, built-in return and different time frames.

Policy with 50% Total Fixed Return

Years to Maturity	Amount Invested	Death Benefit Interest	Simple Effective Annual Rate of Return
1	$100,000	$150,000	50%
2	—	$150,000	25%
3	—	$150,000	16.67%
4	—	$150,000	12.5%
5	—	$150,000	10%
6	—	$150,000	8.33%

Policy with 60% Total Fixed Return

Years to Maturity	Amount Invested	Death Benefit Interest	Simple Effective Annual Rate of Return
1	$100,000	$160,000	60%
2	—	$160,000	30%
3	—	$160,000	20%
4	—	$160,000	15%
5	—	$160,000	12%
6	—	$160,000	10%

Policy with 70% Total Fixed Return

Years to Maturity	Amount Invested	Death Benefit Interest	Simple Effective Annual Rate of Return
1	$100,00	$170,000	70%
2	—	$170,000	35%
3	—	$170,000	23.33%
4	—	$170,000	17.5%
5	—	$170,000	14%
6	—	$170,000	11.67%

Notice from the examples above, that regardless of the year the contract matures, your money increases by the amount you were contractually promised. Essentially you are buying a higher future value with a lower present value dollar and it's locked in contractually. Would it give you peace of mind to know that your money will increase by 50%, 60% or 70% 4-6 years from now or maybe earlier? Or do you like gambling with your money and taking a chance that it will increase or decrease over time. I'm not a gambling man, so I stick to the sure things in life.

I want to do one more comparison to help you understand how powerful this asset can be. Let's compare life settlements to traditional investments with which you are most likely familiar. Let's assume you have $100,000 to save and you want to see how it will perform in a life settlement contract with 60% built-in equity versus the vehicles you've been familiar with your whole life.

The numbers used in the table below are the ac
writing this book.

Account Type	Money Placed	Growth rate	Amount at 5 years	after 5 years
Savings	$100,000	.03% APR	$100,150.11	$150.11
CD	$100,000	1% APR	$105,124.92	$5,124.92
Life Settlement	**$100,000**	**60% Built-in**	**$160,000**	**$60,000**
Stocks	$100,000	No Clue	No Clue	No Clue
Mutual Funds	$100,000	No Clue	No Clue	No Clue

As you can see on the chart above the savings vehicles offered by banks are sub-par and don't even keep up with inflation. Or as one of my clients put it, "I don't even make enough per year with our savings account to take my wife out to a nice dinner."

With stocks and mutual funds the results are unclear and murky. Honestly ask yourself, "Where will my money be 5 years from now, if I keep it in stocks and mutual funds?" Who's to say it won't be less than what you started with 5 years earlier? In 1999 and 2007, investors in Wall Street thought their money would just keep going up forever and ever. Their money was at all-time highs. After the market dropped, they would spend the next 5 years scraping to get back to breakeven. Why lose? Why not have contractual increases that are locked in from the moment you purchase?

With the life settlements your money grew by the contracted amount. In this case, it was 60%. The contract had built-in equity. It's not like the life settlement company is waiting for the stock market to bounce back or the economy to turn around. The company simply collects the death benefit proceeds owed to them by the insurance company. The investor then sees the growth reflected in their account.

Chapter Nine

Spring The Tax Trap

"In this world nothing can be said to be certain, except death and taxes."

--Benjamin Franklin

"You may think you will be in a lower tax bracket later, but you don't know."

--Ed Slott, CPA

One of the main reasons people buy life insurance is because the cash value you grow inside of a policy grows completely tax-free. However, to receive this benefit you have to use after tax dollars.

One of the best features of a life settlement is that you can now buy into the safety, protection and longevity of life insurance with qualified funds. This means you can buy into life insurance using IRA money and old 401k Money. If you are a business owner and don't want to have your SEP IRA in the stock market anymore, you can use it to buy into the safety of a life insurance company.

I am often asked questions regarding the tax benefits of a life settlement. The largest tax benefit actually goes to the seller of the life insurance plan. The seller is able to receive a large portion of their lump sum completely tax-free.

So what are the tax advantages of life settlements to an individual investor? The answer to this question is dependent on the funds used to purchase the contracts.

Let's start with qualified funds such as a 401k, IRA, SEP IRA, 403b or TSA account. All of these accounts at some point can be turned into a self-directed account. By using a self-directed account you as the investor, take control of your own money. You decide how it is invested, not some fund manager on Wall Street whom you'll never meet.

By using qualified funds you are able to use pre-taxed dollars to go to work for you in the life settlement program. You simply move your funds to a self-directed account. Then you guide the account to buy into the contracts you feel will be best suited for you.

This allows you to keep your money growing tax-deferred or tax delayed for a very long time. As you have maturities and see your account grow by 35-80%, your money drops back into your account without creating a taxable event.

You can continue to grow your money tax-deferred for a very long time, but you will need to be conscious of the Required Minimum Distribution or RMDs at age 70 ½. As you near this age, you need to maintain liquidity in one of your qualified accounts to pay Uncle Sam his owed portion.

Through the use of advanced strategies, you can make this much easier by spreading your funds over several policies as you near the RMD phase of your life. This allows smaller amounts to come out more often and creates a pseudo stream of income. This frees up money on a more regular basis to cover RMDs. Speak with me or one of my agents in greater detail about this strategy.

The other advantage most people are unaware of, is something called a stretch IRA or a beneficiary IRA. In the tax code you can assign a beneficiary to receive your IRA funds upon your passing. If they receive your IRA in a lump sum, there will be serious tax consequences. (Make sure you check with your tax advisor when starting this process.)

This is not a product, but a strategy that best-selling author Ed Slott teaches. A beneficiary can continue to have the inherited IRA earn interest and grow without taxes. They will have to pay RMDs on the account. The RMDs are usually small and the earnings of your account can help offset the taxes as you slowly and systematically pull money from the account. This prevents people from paying huge taxes on lump sums and keeps the inherited money growing.

If you're buying into life settlements with cash, the tax burden is a little trickier and involves an upfront disclaimer. I am not a tax accountant. I don't pretend to be one and I don't play a tax advisor on TV or with my clients. I have a tax advisor whom I happily pay to keep me compliant with Uncle Sam.

With that said, you can use cash in a life settlement program. The fees are usually non-existent and there are tax advantages. The biggest tax advantage is being able to pay taxes as you earn. There's no delaying the money you will owe Uncle Sam. Just pay it as you go!

You will only pay tax as you have maturities in your account. Here is where you will need to seek professional tax advice. Most of the tax advisors with whom I have spoken have said, that if a contract matures and pays out after 1 year, the gains are considered capital gains. This would help you pay taxes in a lower tax bracket.

Again, I suggest you speak with a tax professional about this question if you are thinking of using cash. By their very nature, life settlements will usually have a completion time of 2 to 6 years, so understanding the time frame within the capital gains tax rules is important.

Lastly, the very best way to invest in life settlements is with a Roth IRA. With a Roth IRA you are using after tax dollars that will never be taxed again under current IRS tax rules. Imagine being able to contractually increase your retirement and your investment accounts by 35-80% every 3-6 years without having to ever pay tax on that money. Not ever!

By using a Roth you are seeing uninterrupted growth on your account. You are able to use that money completely tax free down the road. The best part is your beneficiary can stretch the Roth IRA and continue to grow their inheritance over their lifetime, too.

Many of the investors I work with make too much money to be able to take advantage of a Roth IRA. You will want to meet with a tax advisor to make sure you fit the requirements.

Even if you don't, there are still ways to legally get your money over into a Roth IRA. Thanks to our government's need for tax money, we have a way to convert traditional IRA money into Roth IRA money. Yes, you have to pay the taxes now, but then you are finished paying taxes on that money forever.

Work with your self-directed IRA fund custodian to systematically work out a schedule for converting IRA funds over to Roth IRA funds over time. This prevents you from being hit with a large tax bill or jumping into a higher income tax bracket each year. Again, work with a great tax advisor on this.

I'm not going to beat around the bush about taxes. I absolutely believe taxes will be higher in the future. A major part of my practice is helping clients build truly tax-free retirement plans through specially designed life insurance because of the tax advantages. Be mindful that Uncle Sam wants to get his hands on as much of your money as he can. Qualified accounts, that have not yet been taxed, are low hanging fruit. By the way, you know he's not really your uncle, right?

Take advantage of the safety and exceptional growth of the life settlement's program, but make sure you keep taxes in the front of your mind. If executed properly, there are tax advantages with the program; you just have to proactively use them.

Bonus tax idea for business owners and the self-employed

There is one more strategy you can use to get the most tax-free growth on your money. You will want to consult with a tax advisor or CPA, but let me give you a 10,000 foot view of how this works. If you are a business owner or are self-employed, you are probably familiar with a SEP IRA.

If you are a successful business owner that makes big money, then you have probably been advised to use a SEP IRA. Perhaps, you were told that you make too much money to contribute to a Roth IRA. This is true advice, but it is open to options.

Maybe it's true that you may make too much money to contribute to a Roth IRA, but you can never make too much money to convert IRA or SEP IRA dollars to a Roth IRA. As of this writing, you can contribute $53,000 a year to a SEP IRA and $5,500 a year to a Roth IRA. (You can contribute $6,500 into a Roth if you are older than 50.)

For the past few years, you have been able, without penalty, to convert IRA dollars to Roth IRA accounts. You just have to pay the taxes. This gives Uncle Sam a way to collect tax dollars without having to wait until a person turns 70 ½.

The premise behind this idea is to fund as much as you can into a SEP IRA each year. Then wait 1 year and convert those dollars or a portion of those dollars over into a Roth account. You won't be able to contribute to the Roth account in the years you earn too much; however, you can always convert dollars as long as you are willing to pay the tax.

For example, let's say you placed $53,000 into your SEP IRA this year. Next year, you could convert the $53,000 over into a Roth IRA and pay the tax. What is the benefit of this strategy? You pay the tax now while tax brackets are historically low and you get those dollars into a Roth that will never be taxed again. It's like getting 9.5 years' worth of Roth contributions in a single year.

You will want to check with your funds custodian, but in the case of life settlements, you can buy the contracts with pre-tax dollars and start the conversion process. Since most life settlement contracts take a couple years to mature, you can have the conversion completed before the maturity occurs, thus receiving tax-free increase on your fund dollars.

Of course you always want to do this in accordance with the IRS tax laws and under the direction of a wise tax advisor. Nothing is illegal if done according to the code. This can also be done with traditional IRA dollars since you can convert those to Roth IRA accounts after paying the tax.

Be mindful of your taxes as your money grows. It's nice to save money by not paying tax up front as you contribute to an IRA or 401k, but it is a pain in the neck to pay taxes during the years you need the money and are no longer working.

If you end up working with me personally or with one of my many agents nationwide, be sure to ask about how to build a tax-free retirement using specially built life insurance. As a bonus, we can even show you how to use the money in your life insurance plan to earn interest in your account and how to make it earn interest in life settlements at the same time. This is a very advanced strategy, reserved for sophisticated investors; however, there is a way to make your money earn interest in both places, at the same time, using these specialized life insurance contracts.

Remember, when it comes to growing and investing your money. you need to understand how the investments work, so you don't lose money or become dependent upon your agents or advisors. After all no one cares about your money as much as you do, except Uncle Sam.

Chapter Ten

Fees: Outwit Wall Street

When it comes to fees, life settlements might be the most cost effective investment around, except for that free checking account you opened in the 80s, when your local bank was handing out toasters. That was a pretty sweet deal!

In every single life settlement conversation with a prospect or client, the question of fees has been brought up. Truth be told, I am usually the one bringing it up because it is such a great selling point for helping people truly compound their money without fees eating into their growth.

This chapter may be hard to read if you have money in the stock market or if you have money in an IRA or 401k. The reality is you are being fee'd to death and don't even know it. Fees are quietly robbing you of your desired future and you don't even know it is happening.

That was the case with one of my clients in Illinois. Let's call him Mike, just to keep his real name anonymous. We had finished moving his money from TD Ameritrade over to his life settlement investment account. Up to this point, Mike was very excited about the program. He had mentioned to me on several occasions how much sense this made to him and that he wished he had found it 20 years earlier.

A few weeks after wrapping up Mike's paperwork I was placing his folder in my filing cabinet when I accidentally dropped the file, exposing several of the pages inside.

Up to that point I had not noticed one of the pages. It was the small print page that discussed what Mike's fees were each year. I read the amount; it was $3,172.04 per year. I couldn't believe it. The fee on his life settlement account was a flat $125 a year. Were we really saving him $3,047 a year in fees? This made me wonder whether I was reading this incorrectly.

I phoned Mike to tell him about the fees I had uncovered on his former fund custodian's paperwork. When I told him the amount, Mike said, "You're kidding me Steve." I wish I had been. Imagine if Mike had gone another 10 years, growing his money with this group, without knowing he was paying thousands of dollars in fees per year.

I will share one more story with you about another client of mine. Let's call him Dr. Baby Maker for this story. After all, my client is a fertility specialist and a really good one at that. As the doctor and I discussed his financial situation, he told me of the unfortunate losses his retirement account had suffered in 2008.

The doctor shared his concerns about further losses and his decision to shift over to safer strategies. I couldn't blame him for being cautious. In fact, I still think he made the right decision to shift his account to a money market account. However, this decision brought with it low to non-existent interest rates. His account simply wasn't growing.

We had to have a long discussion on inflation and places to grow his money outside of Wall Street. At this point the doctor had lost all confidence in the Wall Street casino. This is when we discussed putting a portion of his funds into life settlements. Because of his medical background, the program made a lot of sense. After reviewing the medical information of each contract, the doctor could see that none of the individuals the company had purchased contracts on would live forever.

This brought us to the discussion of fees. At first the doctor protested that he was not paying any fees on his current account. After all, he had never received an invoice or seen a charge on his credit card. I explained to him how the investment company takes the money off the account after crediting his earnings. He could hardly believe a well-known investment group would do such a thing.

The doctor called his investment group to request that his account fees and expenses be disclosed to him. After learning that he was being charged more than $15,000 a year in management fees, he was upset. No wonder his account value had not been growing. He then said, "Imagine if I had never known Steve. I would have paid them hundreds of thousands of dollars in fees over the course of my time with them."

Then I asked the doctor a question, which may have been poorly timed, but was important none the less. I asked, "What has the group done for you this year to deserve a $15,000 fee?"

"Nothing! They have done nothing for me."

I then asked, "During that difficult time in 2008, when you lost nearly half of your hard earned money, did they take their fee while your account was losing?"

He replied, "Yes, they did take their fee; although, it seems a little criminal."

I can't imagine losing any of my clients' money. I always recommend strategies that are safe and have safety precautions built-in to guard against loss. But on the crazy chance that I might lose someone's money, I can't imagine being able to charge their account an exorbitant fee and then look myself in the mirror.

If a restaurant botches your order, they don't charge you. If the dry cleaner ruins your shirt, they buy you a new shirt. If a valet company wrecks your car, their insurance will replace the car or fix the damages. But when Wall Street loses trillions of dollars of their clients' money, they still take their fees and they still issue executive bonuses. It makes me sick!

John Bogle, founder and former CEO of the Vanguard group had this to say about fees: "What happens in the fund business is that the magic of compounding returns is overwhelmed by the tyranny of compounding costs."

In an interview he then continued with a great example of how these seemingly small fees can cut your money in half.

"Okay, let's assume there are two investors: Investor No. 1 owns a portfolio of stocks worth $100,000, pays no ongoing fees (apart from commissions when he purchased his shares) and earns the market return of 7 per cent annually. Investor No. 2 owns the same stocks in a mutual fund that charges 2 per cent in fees, and he therefore earns a return of 5 per cent."

"Now fire up your compounding calculator, because the fun is about to begin. For Investor No. 1, in the box labeled "current principal," enter $100,000. Leave the next box, labeled "annual addition," blank, because we'll assume he doesn't make any additional contributions.

"Now, in the "years to grow" box, enter 50, and for "interest rate," enter 7. In the next box, make sure the calculator is set to "compound interest 1 time(s) annually." Finally, hit "calculate.

"If you've done everything right, you should see a "future value" of $2,945,702.51. This is what Investor No. 1 would end up with after 50 years at a growth rate of 7 per cent. To figure out his return, subtract the original $100,000, which gives you $2,845,702.51.

"Now do the same for Investor No. 2. The only number you need to change is the interest rate, which is now 5 per cent. Hit "calculate," and you'll get a future value of $1,146,739.98, for a return of $1,046,739.98.

"You'll notice that Investor No. 2's return is less than half of Investor No. 1's. In fact, consistent with Mr. Bogle's example, Investor No. 2 made about 63% less than Investor No. 1 – and all because of just 2% in fees charged every year."

As you can see, these ongoing management fees can devour your earnings over time. This is because the management fees hit your entire portfolio and new earnings annually. So as you earn more, and your money hopefully compounds, so do your management fees.

There are 17 hidden fees in 401ks and nearly 20 hidden fees in mutual funds. So how will your money grow over the next 5 to 10 years? With the stock market you never know. You can only speculate and guess. Nothing is contractual. The only thing the big investment houses will put in a contract is how much they will charge you to manage your money, whether it gains or loses. And even that is buried or hidden most of the time.

I think the real sting of fees comes from discovering how much they really are. Most of the people I have helped to uncover their fees are upset to realize just how much they have been spending on annual fees. The thing that seems to really hurt is the fact they feel lied to, or tricked, or purposely kept in the dark. Sometimes we can forgive the wrong, but the lying about the wrong doing is the hardest part to overcome.

This happened with a gentleman in Virginia with whom I was working on a life settlement deal. We went over these same undisclosed fees, and he told me how grateful he was to not be one of the people fooled by fees. I was a little suspect when he told me he wasn't being charged fees. It wasn't that I didn't want to believe him. It's just that I am told that on a weekly basis, and then I am the one left bearing the bad news.

I decided not to push the issue as it seemed he was eager to get involved in the life settlement program. However, about a week later I received an email which was filled with heated words and a sense of urgency to move his money ASAP. This gentleman had just received his annual statement. He found the fee section of his plan. This gentleman was being charged one of the highest fees I had seen in all my years.

The fees listed on his statement were as follows:

Supplement dated March 29th, 2014
Of the Class A shares Prospectus dates January 31st, 2014

Management Fee	1.50%
Distribution 12b-1 Fee	0.00%
Other expenses	0.62%
AFFE Fee	1.42%
Total Annual Fee	3.54%

So how do these small fees really affect your retirement funds growth? Let's say you had $100,000. Let's compare how 1%, 2% and 3% management fees look on your account. Let's also assume your account grows by 5%.

Starting balance	Interest rate earned	Interest Rate after Fees	Annual Percentage Fees
$100,000	5%	4%	1%
$100,000	5%	3%	2%
$100,000	5%	2%	3%

You can see very quickly, how the percent you earn is quickly diluted by the fees you must pay, but it gets worse because you aren't paying the fees on just the earnings. You are paying fees on the total amount managed. The tables below show you how the fees eat into the growth on your account.

1% Annual Management Fee

Account balance	5% Return	1% fee	4% net return
$100,000	$5000	-$1050	$103,950

2% Annual Management Fee

Account balance	5% Return	2% fee	3% net return
$100,000	$5000	-$2100	$102,900

3% Annual Management Fee

Account balance	5% Return	3% fee	2% net return
$100,000	$5000	-$3150	$101,850

You've now seen the tyranny of compounding fees as described by John Bogle. Your fund's custodian will place on your statement or verbally confirm that you have received a 5% increase for the year. The funds custodian will then take off their annual management fee. This happens whether your account increases or decreases.

Can you see why Americans have less money than they should? Can you see why the creator of the 401k said that an annual management fee of just 1% over an employee's career could rob their retirement account of nearly 50%?

The math doesn't lie! This is why the numbers are well guarded and the conversation of fees is avoided at all costs. Let's look at the math just one other way to really drive home how much Wall Street is draining away from your accounts into theirs. In the case of the 1% fee above, the account earned $5,000 and the fee was $1,050. If we take the $1,050 divided by the $5,000 the calculator will show 21%.

This means that the annual management fee ate 21% of your annual return. With the 2% fee $2,100 divided by $5,000 is 42% of your earnings. With the 3% fee of $3,150 divide by $5,000 it is a whopping 63% of your total earnings for the year. Wall Street is eating your growth for breakfast. Up until today, you may have never have known this.

Can you see why former Vanguard CEO, John Bogle says over a career, the saver or investor may end up with 63% less money than what they should have received? It's no wonder, Wall Street is making so much money.

Wall Street takes none of the risk, puts up none of the money and makes the lion's share of the profits. To me this seems like a systemic issue the average investor will never win against.

Now compare this with the flat annual fee of $125 a year for most life settlement investments. This means that whether you are one of our clients who starts with $25,000 or one of our clients that starts with $10,000,000 the fee is a flat $125 per year.

Can you see just from a 'fees eating into your future' stand point, why my client who saved $3000 a year was happy? Why the client who saved over $15,000 a year in fees was happy? Fees are an invisible killer of wealth and fees are one aspect of your retirement plan you can control. Do you know what your fees are?

Don't allow fees to rob you of the money you should have during the accumulation phase of your career and certainly don't allow fees to rob you of the growth and income you will need during your retirement years. You only get one shot at building your nest egg. Control your costs and look for contractual increases on your money. No more speculating or hoping for the retirement of your dreams. With life settlements you have peace of mind that fees aren't eating into your hard earned money and aren't slowing down your growth.

Chapter Eleven

JT's Story: Building A Family Legacy

I want to share one last story with you, because I believe it resonates with a lot of people. This is the story of how JT was introduced into life settlements and how life settlements have changed his life. This story is told by JT, himself.

I grew up in Madison, Wisconsin. I come from a family where both parents worked to provide for our family. My father was raised in a Navy family. My mother is a member of the Bad River Indian Tribe. Both of my parents worked in government positions. Being nearly 7 feet tall, I decided to get into the construction business.

My parents were always incredibly encouraging, so I opened up my own construction company. For 17 years I ran an asphalt and concrete service business. I was doing very well. When my company was at its largest, I had over 100 people working for me. We were cranking out work at an alarming pace. This allowed me to save a lot of money. It also created good cash flow for the business.

As 2007 neared, the economy and the construction market started to soften. I was scrambling to keep over 100 people employed, jobs progressing, and contracts paying us for our work. Around this same time, I started receiving statements from my retirement account. Every month, it seemed, my account balance was bouncing around, but it never seemed to consistently go up. By 2008, the stress of it all was taking a major toll on my health. I was ill every morning before I headed out the door to be the boss and to be sure everyone was paid.

During this time, I had a financial advisor stop by my office to see if he could give me a second opinion on my retirement plan. He introduced me to a new concept called life settlements. I was initially upset that he was interrupting my work day but with the way my savings accounts were going up and down while I tried to maintain a retirement package for my guys, I was open to learning.

We talked for a long time about the ups and downs that I was experiencing. I showed the advisor my statements, so he could better understand my situation. The first thing he pointed out was the high fees I was paying for my brokerage account. He then pointed out that all of my money was in the market and susceptible to loss. I told the advisor I would be willing to look at some safe options; where I knew how my money would grow.

This opened up the conversation about life settlements. He explained to me how it all worked, the safety features of a life insurance company and so forth. It all sounded way too good to be true. I asked him to leave me some reading material and told him I would call him later to talk more.

I immediately contacted my father, who worked in the Wisconsin Public Service Commission regulatory office. I was convinced this was a scam, and I wasn't about to let this guy rip me or anyone else off. I handed over all the materials to my father. I explained to him how the investment alternative worked. My father admitted it sounded legit, but he could understand why I would want more information on it.

This is when my father ran it up the flag pole with an attorney and several of the state financial regulators. Several weeks later, to my surprise, my father called me to tell me that everything had checked out. He asked me how I had come across this opportunity, because traditionally only large institutions with over $100 million in capital could participate. He then said, "Son, I believe this is worth looking into. In fact I wish I had found this 20 years ago."

This gave me a huge boost of confidence. I called the guy that introduced me to the concept and ended up moving money over into a life settlement account. Over time, I was very impressed with everything I had researched and the maturities I was seeing. It gave me enough money to open up a qualified care facility. I had wanted to open a qualified care facility for many years because I am passionate about making sure people get high quality medical care. Besides, my parents are getting older and I wanted to have a way to take care of them someday. After running a qualified care facility, it became very clear how expensive retirement could become. I became very passionate about this strategy and how it could set people up for a good retirement.

After seeing for myself how this program worked, and that no one had lost any money in 2007 and 2008, I set out to introduce the concept to my family members. I wanted to save them from future losses. I wanted to help my family gain back the money they had lost over the years. Ultimately, I was able to assist grandparents, my parents, siblings and cousins.

Now let me say that I was taking a real risk by doing this because I love my family. I didn't want to be the guy, who is shunned at family parties because I shared a financial concept that lost my entire family's money. To this day, each member of my family is very happy with the results.

Now, I offer life settlements to people I meet who qualify. I've been able to help dairy farmers, contractors, commercial real estate agents, and business owners participate in a savings program where they are protected against market loss and will contractually increase their money over time. This has given me and my family peace of mind and a blueprint for how to grow our money. We now teach our kids to do the same so they can avoid the stress and setbacks that come with losing money.

Life settlements have been a God send in my own life and the life of my family. Today I now own two qualified care facilities in Wisconsin and hope to be able to share even more in my community. Life settlements just make sense to me and now after 7 years of personal experience, they still make more sense to me than any other investment vehicle I have come across.

Chapter Twelve

Peace Of Mind Planning

"Make it a must that whenever you hear about
something, read or research something you
think has value for your life, don't let it
become knowledge. Convert it into action,
for it is through actions that our destiny is shaped."

--Tony Robbins

One of the most satisfying experiences of my career has been calling clients to tell them there has been a maturity. To tell them their accounts will be increasing within the next week. For clients to hear that their account value is going to see the contractual increase we discussed when they first came on board is exciting.

The other satisfying aspect of what I do has come from getting phone calls during distressing times to make sure a clients' money is not losing or dropping in value. I remember one such call that came in the Fall of 2013. The US government had been shut down for over 10 days. The stock market was dropping and the news was all about our country defaulting on payments to China. It was a scary time.

My client called to make sure his account was safe. He reminded me that I had told him that if the markets dropped, his account would be safe. He reminded me that when the stock market dropped by $300 billion in 2011 after the earthquake in Japan that I said no one had lost money in their life settlement accounts.

I could tell he was scared because his portfolio lost over 40% in 2008 and he was not looking forward to receiving bad news again. We got on the computer together and looked up his account. While we were pulling up his account, I reminded him of how his money was not in the stock market. That his earnings were not linked to the performance or health of the economy, the jobs report or the consumer confidence report.

I reminded my client that his funds were in an irrevocable trust that had ownership in several "A" rated life insurance companies contracts and that his payout was linked to these contracts and the financial well-being of these companies. This seemed to jog his memory and put him at ease. Still, I pulled up his account, so we could look at it together.

The account finally pulled up and my client could see that his money was all there. He could see that, although the stock market had dropped, his account value had not. We then looked over his contracts, the time frame and how they would grow contractually.

This gave my client peace of mind. He told me how he started to relive 2008. Seeing the stock market drop had conjured up all the stress and fear he had back then. It made me feel good to know that my client had protected his money and that he knew how it would grow. I look forward to calling this particular client in the near future to tell him that his money has seen an increase and to show him it is the amount he expected when he signed up.

I have tremendous peace of mind knowing that my clients have money inside vehicles they can understand. Understanding how investments work is empowering, and is crucial for success. I hope this book has given you an understanding of how this powerful asset class works. I know this strategy is not for everyone and not everyone will qualify to use it, but the clients that have moved forward have been very happy they did.

So where do you go from here?

I believe you owe it to yourself to better understand how this asset can benefit your retirement, your peace of mind and your future. You have nothing to lose by learning more about life settlements and everything to gain.

Most of the companies I have relationships with, are willing to educate you on their process and show you the contracts they have available. In fact, with most of them you can see dollar for dollar how your money will contractually increase before you ever sign any papers or place a single dime in an account. Very few investments can show you a glimpse of your future. Even fewer can give you the peace of mind that it will come to fruition.

See how your money will grow. Better understand why the largest banks, investment groups and hedge funds are buying billions of dollars of life settlement contracts. Better understand how they are using it with the money they are not willing to risk in the market and how it balances out their portfolio.

See for yourself and your family, how this could be a huge stress reliever. Free up the time you used to spend watching MSNBC and Cramer to guess what the next hot stock will be. Take back the time you spend on Yahoo Finance looking for P/E ratios and undervalued stocks.

Remember that a rising tide lifts all boats and a lowering tide reveals who has been swimming naked. With the Fed printing billions of dollars every month to place in the stock market, we are seeing a rising tide, albeit, an artificial rising of the tide. When the markets dropped in 2008, it pulled down nearly every account with the exception of insurance based products not correlated with the stock market. The tides are sinking. Don't get caught naked!

Warning!

It is human nature when we first hear about a new concept that resonates with us to first imagine how this could benefit us or someone we care about.

The second reaction is to go back to our normal routine or to what we feel is most comfortable. This is natural, but not necessarily good. If you are reading this book it is because you have probably suffered retirement account losses in the past and you want a better way of growing your money. Doing what was considered traditional or accepted by the masses is what got most of us in trouble in the first place.

Peace of mind

What is it you are really after with your investments? Isn't it really peace of mind? You want to know with certainty that you will be able to retire. You want to know that you won't lose money again. You want to be able to dream and make plans for your future.

Investing in the stock market has made peace of mind next to impossible. The stock market has robbed more Americans of their dreams than any other thing. It doesn't have to be this way. You can control your future and you can invest in predictable assets.

Life settlements provide peace of mind to investors that they can grow their money contractually. Having a contract in place on how your money will grow should be a requirement of all investments. Would you take a new job and work for a year not knowing what you would be paid? No contractor breaks ground on a new building without knowing their client can pay them and how much they will be paid. Having a contract in place is a sound business practice.

Buying equity in contracts offered by the largest, most stable guardians of wealth, gives significant peace of mind. Having ownership in a contract with an "A" rate life insurance company, gives peace of mind. These companies have been keeping their commitments and promises to the American people for over 100 years. Their track record is unbeatable and solid.

Don't we buy insurance to give us peace of mind, that if our car is wrecked or our house burns down, that the insurance company will make it right? That we are in good hands and like a good neighbor they will be there for us? So why not use the insurance industry to safely and predictably increase your wealth. The banks have used this blueprint for over 100 years.

Let us design you a peace of mind blueprint, a financial blueprint that ends with you having your money safe and growing, a blueprint that takes away the worry of guessing whether the market will crash this month or next. Walk away from the gambling and take away the speculating. Wall Street and casinos are set up to make sure the house wins; no matter how many people have to lose to make it happen. Let us model the bank's billion dollar blueprint for you and give you a solid investment plan to contractually grow your wealth just like the banks.

Let us answer your questions about life settlements. Let us show you the value of this asset class. Let us show you how your money will grow and the peace of mind that comes from not having to worry or dwell for a single second more on what the stock market is doing.

Begin your peace of mind blueprint by planning to work with the agent or advisor who gave you this book. If it was given to you it's because the agent felt this strategy would be a good fit for your financial situation. Giving this book to you says something about the agent you are working with. They are most likely well-read and continually educating themselves for their clients benefit. Start by asking how this strategy could benefit your personal situation and then let them explain the ins and outs of this truly unique asset. Finally, proceed to looking at the contracts and companies they represent and how your money will safely and contractually grow dollar-for-dollar in a life settlement investment. Let this win-win investment safely carry you to your retirement dreams and the peace of mind you are seeking.

Acknowledgments

Writing on a topic you are passionate about is daunting. On the one hand, you feel you are the best person to cover the subject. On the other hand, you wonder if the book will accurately articulate the incredible advantages of teaching people how to safely grow their money outside of Wall Street.

It's not easy to run a national, multi-million dollar company and still find time to write a book. I want to thank all of the people who have brought me to this point in my life, where writing this book was possible. I hope this book will have a huge impact on the way people look at their precious retirement dollars. I hope it will increase their understanding of ways to save outside of the mainstream methods.

First and for most, I want to thank my wife Kacey for being my greatest supporter, not only with writing this book, but in my life. Thank you for putting up with the late nights and early mornings. Thank you for the times I checked out momentarily to write down a thought or copy down an idea. Thank you, Kacey, for everything.

Thank you to my children who are the reasons for working as hard as I do. I hope to not only be a strong support for you to lean on in life, but to arm you with the necessary information that you will need to be successful in life.

Thank you to my parents who have raised me up right and who have taught me good financial principles, since I was a child. Thank you for giving me independence and support throughout my whole life. You have given me the courage to become a business owner; which has stretched me and made me grow more than any other thing in my life. Thank you for encouraging me to be a lifelong learner and seeing me for who I would become.

Thank you to Brian Lund, for giving me the motivation and example to write this book. Thank you for answering my late night and early morning text messages. You have been an incredible partner in brainstorming ideas and concepts. You are a great friend!

Thank you, Mark Maiewski, for inspiring and cultivating many of the million dollar ideas you have given me. Thank you for the encouragement you have given all along the way and will continue to give. Your voice kept me pushing when I wanted to give up on this book. Your insight and wisdom is invaluable.

Thank you to my assistant, Samantha Ahlmer, who keeps my schedule and calendar running smoothly.

Thank you to JT and Jessica McDonald, and your entire staff for your support in building my team and writing this book. Thank you, JT, for not giving up when things were so difficult. I would not be in this business today without you and your constant support. Thank you for being a mentor.

Thank you, Rick and Carol Rust, for everything you do for me. Your understanding of this powerhouse asset has helped me overcome a learning curve faster than I thought possible. Your help has been crucial to my personal success, and to the success of my organization and team. I would not be where I am today, without your help and mentoring.

A special thanks to Jeff Hays and Julie Anderson for all of the support you have given me over the past decade. Your encouragement and vision of my future was strong enough to make me see it for myself and that has made an incredible impact on my life.

About The Author

Stephen Gardner is a Safe Money Specialist that lives in Salt Lake City, Utah with his wife and 3 children. He is also a National Sales Trainer and speaker in the financial services industry. He has often been heard saying "I am on a mission to strengthen America one family at a time." He is passionate about helping families get safe returns on their retirement funds. Although he calls himself Stephen, many of his clients and friends call him Safe Money Steve.

Stephen is also the founder of the Safe Millionaire Club. The Safe Millionaire Club has millionaire and multi-millionaire members all over the world. The group is dedicated to educating its members on sound financial principles and safe money strategies. To learn about becoming a member or to be a part of the group's retreats, contact the author's office for additional information.

Get a Personalized Blueprint and work with the author or his team

To get a personalized blueprint and see how your money will grow and be protected in the life settlement program, contact our office today to schedule a time to speak with a life settlement specialist. Let us show you available contracts and explain how this unique investment would benefit your unique situation.

Contact us at SafeMillionaireClub@gmail.com or 888-638-0080.

Made in the USA
Lexington, KY
26 February 2015